THREE CONTRIBUTIONS TO THE SEXUAL THEORY

BY

PROF. SIGMUND FREUD, LL.D.,

VIENNA.

AUTHORIZED TRANSLATION

BY

A. A. BRILL, Ph.B., M.D.,

CLINICAL ASSISTANT DEPARTMENT OF PSYCHIATRY AND NEUROLOGY, COLUMBIA UNIVERSITY ;
ASSISTANT IN MENTAL DISEASES, BELLEVUE HOSPITAL, ASSISTANT VISITING PHYSICIAN,
HOSPITAL FOR NERVOUS DISEASES

WITH INTRODUCTION

BY

JAMES J. PUTNAM, M.D.

I0123291

ISBN: 978-1-63182-881-2

Printed: March 2023

Published and Distributed By:
Lushena Books
607 Country Club Drive, Unit E
Bensenville, IL 60106
www.lushenabks.com

ISBN: 978-1-63182-881-2

TABLE OF CONTENTS

AUTHOR'S PREFACE TO THE SECOND EDITION

Although the author is fully aware of the gaps and obscurities contained in this small volume, he has, nevertheless, resisted a temptation to add to it the results obtained from the investigations of the last five years, fearing that thus its unified and documentary character would be destroyed. He accordingly reproduces the original text with but slight modifications, contenting himself with the addition of a few footnotes. For the rest, it is his ardent wish that this book may speedily become antiquated—to the end that the new material brought forward in it may be universally accepted, while the shortcomings it displays may give place to juster views.

VIENNA, December, 1909.

INTRODUCTION TO TRANSLATION

The somewhat famous "Three Essays" which Dr. Brill is here bringing to the attention of an English-reading public, occupy—brief as they are—an important position among the achievements of their author, a great investigator and pioneer in an important line. It is not claimed that the facts here gathered are altogether new. The subject of the sexual instinct and its aberrations has long been before the scientific world and the names of many effective toilers in this vast field are known to every student. When one passes beyond the strict domains of science and considers what is reported of the sexual life in folk-lore and art-lore and the history of primitive culture and in romance, the sources of information are immense. Freud has made considerable additions to this stock of knowledge, but he has done also something of far greater consequence than this. He has worked out, with incredible penetration, the part which this instinct plays in every phase of human life and in the development of human character, and has been able to establish on a firm footing the remarkable thesis that psychoneurotic illnesses never occur with a perfectly normal sexual life. Other sorts of emotions contribute to the result, but some abnormality of the sexual life is always present, as the cause of especially insistent emotions and repressions.

The instincts with which every child is born furnish desires or cravings which must be dealt with in some fashion. They may be refined ("sublimated"), so far as is necessary and desirable, into energies of other sorts—as happens readily with the play-instinct—or they may remain as the source of perversions and inversions, and of cravings of new sorts substituted for those of the more primitive kinds under the pressure of a conventional civilization. The symptoms of the functional psychoneuroses represent, after a fashion, one of these inadequate attempts to find a substitute for the imperative cravings born of the sexual instincts, and their form often depends, in part at least, on the peculiarities of the sexual life in infancy and early childhood. It is Freud's service to have investigated this inadequately chronicled period of existence with extraordinary acumen. In so doing he made it plain that the "perversions" and "inversions" which reappear later under such striking shapes, belong to the normal sexual life of the young child and are seen, in veiled forms, in almost every case of nervous illness.

It cannot too often be repeated that these discoveries represent no fanciful deductions, but are the outcome of rigidly careful observations which any one who will sufficiently prepare himself can verify. Critics fret over the amount of "sexuality" that Freud finds evidence of in the histories of his patients, and assume that he puts it there. But such criticisms are evidences of misunderstandings and proofs of ignorance.

Freud had learned that the amnesias of hypnosis and of hysteria were not absolute but relative and that in covering the lost memories, much more, of unexpected sort, was often found. Others, too, had gone as far as this, and stopped. But this investigator determined that nothing but the absolute impossibility of going further should make him cease from urging his patients into an inexorable scrutiny of the unconscious regions of their memories and thoughts, such as never had been made before. Every species of forgetfulness, even the forgetfulness of childhood's years, was made to yield its hidden stores of knowledge; dreams, even though apparently absurd, were found to be interpreters of a varied class of thoughts, active, although repressed as out of harmony with the selected life of consciousness; layer after layer. new sets of motives underlying motives were laid bare, and each patient's interest was strongly enlisted in the task of learning to know himself in order more truly and wisely to "sublimate" himself.

Gradually other workers joined patiently in this laborious undertaking, which now stands, for those who have taken pains to comprehend it, as by far the most important movement in psychopathology.

It must, however, be recognized that these essays, of which Dr. Brill has given a translation that cannot but be timely, concerns a subject which is not only important but unpopular. Few physiciaus read the works of v. Krafft-Ebing, Magnus Hirschfeld, Moll, and others of like sort. The remarkable volumes of Havelock Ellis were refused publication in his native England. The sentiments which inspired this hostile attitude towards the study of the sexual life are still active, though growing steadily less common. One may easily believe that if the facts which Freud's truth-seeking researches forced him to recognize and to publish had not been of an unpopular sort, his rich and abundant contributions to observational psychology, to the significance of dreams, to the etiology and therapeutics of the psychoneuroses, to the interpretation of mythology, would have won for him, by universal acclaim, the same recognition among all physicians that he has received from a rapidly increasing band of followers and colleagues.

May Dr. Brill's translation help toward this end.

There are two further points on which some comments should be made. The first is this, that those who conscientiously desire to learn all that they can from Freud's remarkable contributions should not be content to read any one of them alone. His various publications, such as " The Selected Papers on Hysteria and Other Psychoneuroses,"[1] " The Interpretation of Dreams," " The Psychopathology of Everyday Life," " Wit and its Relation to the Unconscious,"[2] the analysis of the case of the little boy

---

[1] Translated by A. A. Brill, NERVOUS AND MENTAL DISEASE, Monograph Series, No. 4.

[2] Translations of these books in preparation.

called Hans, the study of Leonardo da Vinci, and the various short essays in the two Sammlungen kleiner Schriften, not only all hang together, but supplement each other to a remarkable extent. Unless a course of study such as this is undertaken many critics may think various statements and inferences in this volume to be far fetched or find them too obscure for comprehension.

The other point is the following: One frequently hears the psychoanalytic method referred to as if it was customary for those practicing it to exploit the sexual experiences of their patients and nothing more, and the insistence on the details of the sexual life, presented in this book, is likely to emphasize that notion. But the fact is, as every thoughtful inquirer is aware, that the whole progress of civilization, whether in the individual or the race, consists largely in a " sublimation " of infantile instincts, and especially certain portions of the sexual instinct, to other ends than those which they seemed designed to serve. Art and poetry are fed on this fuel and the evolution of character and mental force is largely of the same origin. All the forms which this sublimation, or the abortive attempts at sublimation, may take in any given case, should come out in the course of a thorough psychoanalysis. It is not the sexual life alone, but every interest and every motive, that must be inquired into by the physician who is seeking to obtain all the data about the patient, necessary for his reëducation and his cure. But all the thoughts and emotions and desires and motives which appear in the man or woman of adult years were once crudely represented in the obscure instincts of the infant, and among these instincts those which were concerned directly or indirectly with the sexual emotions, in a wide sense, are certain to be found in every case to have been the most important for the end-result.

JAMES J. PUTNAM.

BOSTON, August 23, 1910.

THE SEXUAL ABERRATIONS[1]

The fact of sexual need in man and animal is expressed in biology by the assumption of a " sexual impulse." This impulse is made analogous to the impulse of taking nourishment, and to hunger. The sexual expression corresponding to hunger not being found colloquially, science uses the expression "libido."[2]

Popular conception assumes very different ideas concerning the nature and qualities of this sexual impulse. It is supposed to be absent during childhood and to commence about the time of and in connection with the maturing process of puberty; it is supposed that it manifests itself in irresistible attractions exerted by one sex upon the other, and that its aim is sexual union or at least such actions as would lead to union.

But we have every reason to see in these assumptions a very untrustworthy picture of reality. On closer examination they are found to abound in errors, inaccuracies and hasty conclusions.

If we introduce two terms and call the person from whom the sexual attraction emanates the sexual object, and the action towards which the impulse strives the sexual aim, then the scientifically examined experience shows us many deviations in refer-

[1] The facts contained in the first "Contribution" have been gathered from the familiar publications of Krafft-Ebing, Moll, Moebius, Havelock Ellis, Schrenk-Notzing, Löwenfeld, Eulenberg, J. Bloch, and M. Hirschfeld, and from the later works published in the "Jahrbuch für sexuelle Zwischenstufen." As these publications also mention the other literature bearing on this subject I may forbear giving detailed references.

The conclusions reached through the investigation of sexual inverts are all based on the reports of J. Sadger and on my own experience.

[2] For general use the word "libido" is best translated by " craving." (Prof. James J. Putnam, Journal of Abnormal Psychology, Vol. IV, 6.)

ence to both sexual object and sexual aim, the relations of which to the accepted standard require thorough investigation.

I. DEVIATION IN REFERENCE TO THE SEXUAL OBJECT

The popular theory of the sexual impulse corresponds closely to the poetic fable of dividing the person into two halves—man and woman—who strive to become reunited through love. It is therefore very surprising to hear that there are men for whom the sexual object is not woman but man, and that there are women for whom it is not man but woman. Such persons are called contrary sexuals, or better, inverts; that is, these form the actualities of inversion. They exist in very considerable numbers, although their definite ascertainment is subject to difficulties.[3]

A. *Inversion*

The Behavior of Inverts.—The above-mentioned persons behave in many ways quite differently.

(*a*) They are absolutely inverted; *i. e.,* their sexual object must be always of the same sex, while the opposite sex can never be to them an object of sexual longing, but leaves them indifferent or may even evoke sexual repugnance. As men they are unable, on account of this repugnance, to perform the normal sexual act or miss all pleasure in its performance.

(*b*) They are amphigenously inverted (psychosexually hermaphroditic); *i. e.,* their sexual object may belong indifferently to either the same or to the other sex. The inversion lacks the character of exclusiveness.

(*c*) They are occasionally inverted; *i. e.,* under certain external conditions, chief among which are the inaccessibility of the normal sexual object and imitation, they are able to take as the sexual object a person of the same sex and thus find sexual gratification.

[3] For the difficulties entailed in the attempt to ascertain the proportional number of inverts compare the work of M. Hirschfeld in the Jahrbuch für sexuelle Zwischenstufen, 1904.

The inverted also manifest a manifold behavior in their judgment about the peculiarities of their sexual impulse. Some take the inversion as a matter of course, just as the normal looking at his libido does, firmly demanding the same rights as the normal. Others, however, strive against the fact of their inversion and perceive in it a morbid compulsion.[4]

Other variations concern the relations of time. The characteristics of the inversion in any individual may date back as far as his memory goes, or they may become manifest to him at a definite period before or after puberty.[5] The character is either retained throughout life, or it occasionally recedes or represents an episode on the road to normal development. A periodical fluctuation between the normal and the inverted sexual object has also been observed. Of special interest are those cases in which the libido changes, taking on the character of inversion after a painful experience with the normal sexual object.

These different categories of variation generally exist independently of one another. In the most extreme cases it can regularly be assumed that the inversion has existed at all times and that the person feels contented with his peculiar state.

Many authors will hesitate to gather into a unit all the cases enumerated here and will prefer to emphasize the exceptional rather than the customary groups, a view which corresponds with their preferred judgment of inversions. But no matter what divisions may be set up, it cannot be overlooked that all transi-

---

[4] Such a striving against the compulsion to inversion favors cures by suggestion or psychoanalysis.

[5] Many have justly emphasized the fact that the autobiographic statements of inverts, as to the time of the appearance of their tendency to inversion, are untrustworthy as they may have repressed from memory any evidences of heterosexual feelings.

Psychoanalysis has confirmed this suspicion in all cases of inversion accessible, and has decidedly changed their anamnesis by filling up the infantile amnesias.

tions are abundantly met with, so that as it were, the formation of series forcibly obtrudes itself.

Conception of Inversion.—The first attention bestowed upon inversion gave rise to the conception that it was a congenital sign of nervous degeneration. This harmonized with the fact that doctors first met it among the nervous, or among persons giving such an impression. There are two elements which should be considered independently in this conception: the congenitality, and the degeneration.

Degeneration.—This term *degeneration* is open to the objections which may be urged against the promiscuous use of this word in general. It has in fact become customary to designate all morbid manifestations not of traumatic or infectious origin as degenerative. Indeed, Magnan's classification of degenerates makes it conceivable that the highest general configuration of nervous accomplishment need not exclude the application of the concept of degeneration. Under the circumstances it is a question what use and what new content the meaning of " degeneration" still possesses. It would seem more appropriate not to speak of degeneration: (1) Where there are not many marked deviations from the normal; (2) where the capabilities and the capacity to exist do not in general appear markedly impaired.[*]

That the inverted are not degenerates in this qualified sense can be seen from the following facts:

1. The inversion is found among persons who otherwise show no marked deviation from the normal.

2. It is found also among persons whose capabilities are not

[*] With what reserve the diagnosis of degeneration should be made and what slight practical significance can be attributed to it can be gathered from the discussions of Moebius (Ueber Entartung; Grenzfragen des Nerven- und Seelenlebens, No. III, 1900). He says: " If we review the wide sphere of degeneration upon which we have here turned some light we can conclude without further ado that it is really of little value to diagnose degeneration."

disturbed, who on the contrary are distinguished by especially high intellectual development and ethical culture.[7]

3. If one disregards the patients of one's own practice and strives to comprehend a wider field of experience, he will in two directions encounter facts which will prevent him from assuming inversions as a degenerative sign.

(*a*) It must be considered that inversion was a frequent manifestation among the ancient nations at the height of their culture. It was an institution endowed with important functions. (*b*) It is found to be unusually prevalent among savages and primitive races, whereas the term degeneration is generally limited to higher civilization (I. Bloch). Even among the most civilized nations of Europe, climate and race have a most powerful influence on the distribution of, and attitude toward, inversion.[8]

Innateness.—Only for the first and most extreme class of inverts, as can be imagined, has innateness been claimed, and this from their own assurance that at no time in their life has their sexual impulse followed a different course. The fact of the existence of two other classes, especially of the third, speaks against the assumption of its being congenital. Hence, the propensity of those holding this view to separate the group of absolute inverts from the others results in the abandonment of the general conception of inversion. Accordingly in a number of cases the inversion would be of a congenital character, while in others it might originate from other causes.

[7] We must agree with the spokesman of "Uranism" that some of the most prominent men known have been inverts and perhaps absolute inverts.

[8] In the conception of inversion the pathological features have been separated from the anthropological. For this credit is due to J. Bloch (Beiträge zur Ätiologie der Psychopathia Sexualis, 2 Teile, 1902–3) who has also brought into prominence the existence of inversion in the old civilized nations.

In contradistinction to this conception is that which assumes inversion to be an acquired character of the sexual impulse. It is based on the following facts. (1) In many inverts (even absolute ones) an early effective sexual impression can be demonstrated, as a result of which the homosexual inclination developed. (2) In many others outer favoring and inhibiting influences of life can be demonstrated, which in earlier or later life led to a fixation of the inversion—among which are exclusive relations with the same sex, companionship in war, detention in prison, dangers of hetero-sexual intercourse, celibacy, sexual weakness, etc. (3) Hypnotic suggestion may remove the inversion, which would be surprising in that of a congenital character.

In view of all this, the existence of congenital inversion can certainly be questioned. The objection may be made to it that a more accurate examination of those claimed to be congenitally inverted will probably show a determination of the direction of the libido by a definite experience of early childhood, which has not, indeed, been retained in the conscious memory of the person, but which can be brought back to memory by proper influences (Havelock Ellis). According to that author inversion can be designated only as a frequent variation of the sexual desire which may be determined by a number of external circumstances of life.

The apparent certainty thus reached is, however, overthrown by the retort that manifestly there are many persons who have experienced even in their early youth those very sexual influences, such as seduction, mutual onanism, without becoming inverts, or without constantly remaining so. Hence, one is forced to assume that the alternative between congenital and acquired inversion is either incomplete or does not cover the circumstances present in inversions.

Explanation of Inversion.—The nature of inversion is explained by neither the assumption that it is congenital or that it is acquired. In the first case, we need to be told what there is in it of the congenital, unless we are satisfied with the roughest explanation, namely, that a person brings along a congenital sexual desire connected with a definite sexual object. In the second case it is a question whether the manifold accidental influences suffice to explain the acquisition unless there is something in the individual to meet them half way. The negation of this last factor is inadmissible according to our former conclusions.

The Relation of Bisexuality.—Since the time of Frank Lydston, Kiernan, and Chevalier, a new stream of thought has been introduced for the explanation of the possibility of sexual inversion. This contains a new contradiction to the popular belief which assumes that a human being is either a man or a woman. Science shows cases in which the sexual characteristic appears blurred and thus the sexual distinction is made difficult, especially on an anatomical basis. The genitals of such persons unite the male and female characteristics (hermaphroditism). In rare cases both parts of the sexual apparatus are well developed (true hermaphroditism), but usually both are stunted.[9]

The importance of these abnormalities lies in the fact that they unexpectedly facilitate the understanding of the normal formation. A certain degree of anatomical hermaphroditism really belongs to the normal. In no normally formed male or female are traces of the apparatus of the other sex lacking; these either continue functionless as rudimentary organs, or they are transformed for the purpose of assuming other functions.

The conception which we gather from this long known anatomical fact is the original predisposition to bisexuality, which in the course of development has changed to monosexuality, leaving slight remnants of the stunted sex.

[9] Compare the last detailed discussion of somatic hermaphroditism (Taruffi, Hermaphroditismus und Zeugungunfähigkeit, German edit. by R. Teuscher, 1903), and the works of Neugebauer in many volumes of the Jahrbuch für sexuelle Zwischenstufen.

2

It was natural to transfer this conception to the psychic sphere and to conceive the inversion in its aberrations as an expression of psychic hermaphroditism.   In order to bring the question to a decision, it was only necessary to have one other circumstance, viz., a regular concurrence of the inversion with the psychic and somatic signs of hermaphroditism.

But the expectation thus formed was not realized.· The relations between the assumed psychical and the demonstrable anatomical androgyny should never be conceived as being so close. There is frequently found in the inverted a diminution of the sexual impulse (H. Ellis) and a slight anatomical stunting of the organs.   This, however, is found frequently but by no means regularly or preponderately.   Thus we must recognize that inversion and somatic hermaphroditism are totally independent of each other.

Great value has also been placed on the so-called secondary and tertiary sex characteristics, and their aggregate occurrence in the inverted has been emphasized (H. Ellis).   There is much truth in this but it should not be forgotten that the secondary and tertiary sex characteristics very frequently manifest themselves in the other sex, thus indicating androgyny without, however, involving changes in the sexual object in the sense of an inversion.

Psychic hermaphroditism would gain in substantiality if parallel with the inversion of the sexual object there should be at least a change in the other psychic qualities, such as in the impulses and distinguishing traits characteristic of the other sex. But such inversion of character can be expected with some regularity only in inverted women; in men the most perfect psychic manliness may be united with the inversion.   If one firmly adheres to the hypothesis of a psychic hermaphroditism, one must add that in certain spheres its manifestations allow the recognition of only a very slight contrary determination.   The same also holds true in the somatic androgyny.   According to Halban, the appearance of individual stunted organs and secondary sex character are quite independent of each other.[10]

A spokesman of the masculine inverts stated the bisexual theory in its crudest form in the following words: " It is a female brain in a male body." But we do not know the characteristics of a " female brain." The substitution of the anatomical for the psychological is as frivolous as it is unjustified. The attempted explanation by v. Krafft-Ebing seems to be more precisely formulated than that of Ulrich but does not essentially differ from it. v. Krafft-Ebing thinks that the bisexual predisposition gives to the individual male and female brain cells as well as somatic sexual organs. These centers develop first towards puberty mostly under the influence of the independent sex glands. We can, however, say the same of the male and female " centers " as of the male and female brains; and moreover, we do not even know whether we can assume for the sexual functions separate brain locations (" centers ") such as we may assume for language.

After this discussion, two thoughts, as it were, remain; first, that a bisexual predisposition is to be presumed for the inversion also, only we do not know wherein it exists beyond the anatomical formations; and, second, that we are dealing with disturbances which are experienced by the sexual impulse during its development.[11]

[10] J. Halban, " Die Entstehung der Geschlechts Charaktere," Arch. für Gynäkologie, Bd. 70, 1903. See also there the literature on the subject.

[11] According to a report in Vol. 6 of the Jahrbuch f. sexuelle Zwischenstufen, E. Gley is supposed to have been the first to mention bisexuality as an explanation of inversion. He published a paper (Les Abérrations de l'instinct Sexuel) in the Revue Philosophique as early as January, 1884. It is moreover noteworthy that the majority of authors who trace the inversion to bisexuality assume this factor not only for the inverts but also for those who have developed normally, and justly interpret the inversion as a result of a disturbance in development. Among these authors are Chevalier (Inversion Sexuelle, 1893), and v. Krafft-Ebing (" Zur Erklärung der konträren Sexualempfindung," Jahrbücher f. Psy-

The Sexual Object of Inverts.—The theory of psychic herma-phroditism presupposed that the sexual object of the inverted is the reverse of the normal. The inverted man, like the woman, succumbs to the charms emanating from manly qualities of body and mind; he feels himself like a woman and seeks a man.

But however true this may be for a great number of inverts it by no means indicates the general character of inversion. There is no doubt that a great part of the male inverted have retained the psychic character of virility, that proportionately they show but little the secondary characters of the other sex, and that they really look for real feminine psychic features in their sexual object. If that were not so it would be incomprehensible why masculine prostitution, in offering itself to inverts, copies in all its exterior, to-day as in antiquity, the dress and attitudes of woman. This imitation would otherwise be an insult to the ideal of the inverts. Among the Greeks, where the most manly men were found among inverts, it is quite obvious that it was not the mas-culine character of the boy which kindled the love of man, but it was his physical resemblance to woman as well as his feminine psychic qualities, such as shyness, demureness, and the need of

chiatrie u. Nervenheilkunde, XII) who states that there are a number of observations "from which at least the virtual and continued existence of this second center (of the underlying sex) results." A Dr. Arduin (Die Frauenfrage und die sexuellen Zwischenstufen, 2d vol. of the Jahrbuch f. sexuelle Zwischenstufen, 1900) states that "in every man there exist male and female elements." See also the same Jahrbuch, Bd. I, 1899 ("Die objektive Diagnose der Homosexualitat" by M. Hirschfeld, pp. 8-9). In the determination of sex, as far as heterosexual persons are concerned some are disproportionately more strongly developed than others. G. Herman is firm in his belief "that in every woman there are male, and in every man there are female germs and qualities" (Genesis, das Gesetz der Zeugung, 9 Bd., Libido und Manie, 1903). As recently as 1906 has W. Fliess (Der Ablauf des Lebens) claimed ownership of the idea of bisexuality (in the sense of double sex).

instruction and help.   As soon as the boy himself became a man
he ceased to be a sexual object for men and in turn became a
lover of boys.   The sexual object in this case as in many others
is therefore not of the like sex, but it unites both sex characters,
a compromise between the impulses striving for the man and for
the woman, but firmly conditioned by the masculinity of body
(the genitals).[12]

The conditions in the woman are more definite; here the active
inverts, with special frequency, show the somatic and psychic
characters of man and desire femininity in their sexual object;
though even here greater variation will be found on more intimate investigation.

The Sexual Aim of Inverts.—The important fact to bear in
mind is that no uniformity of the sexual aim can be attributed

[12] Although psychoanalysis has not yet given us a full explanation for
the origin of inversion, it has revealed the psychic mechanism of its
genesis and has essentially enriched the problems in question.   In all the
cases examined we have ascertained that the later inverts go through in
their childhood a phase of very intense but short-lived fixation on the
woman (usually on the mother) and after overcoming it they identify
themselves with the woman and take themselves as the sexual object; that
is, following narcissism they look for young men resembling themselves
in person who shall love them as their mother has loved them.   We
have, moreover, frequently found that alleged inverts are by no means
indifferent to the charms of women, but the excitation evoked by the
woman is always transferred to a male object.   They thus repeat through
life the mechanism which gave origin to their inversion.   Their obsessive
striving for the man proves to be determined by their restless flight from
the woman.   It must be remembered, however, that until now only one
type of inversion has been subjected to psychoanalysis, viz., that of persons with a general stunted sexual activity, the remnant of which manifested itself as inversion.   The problem of inversion is very complex and
embraces many diverse types of sexual activity and development.   No-
tionally it should be strictly distinguished whether the inversion reverses
the sex character of the object or of the subject.

to inversion. Intercourse per anum in men by no means goes with inversion; masturbation is just as frequently the exclusive aim; and the limitation of the sexual aim to mere effusion of feelings is here even more frequent than in hetero-sexual love. In women, too, the sexual aims of the inverted are manifold, among which contact with the mucous membrane of the mouth seems to be preferred.,

Conclusion.—Though from the material on hand we are by no means in a position satisfactorily to explain the origin of inversion, we can say that through this investigation we have obtained an insight which can become of greater significance to us than the solution of the above problem. Our attention is called to the fact that we have assumed a too close connection between the sexual impulse and the sexual object. The experience gained from the so called abnormal cases teaches us that there exists between the sexual impulse and the sexual object a connection which we are in danger of overlooking in the uniformity of normal states where the impulse seems to bring with it the object. We are thus instructed to fix our attention upon this connection between the impulse and the object. The sexual impulse is probably entirely independent of its object and does not depend on the stimuli of the same for its origin.

B. *The Sexually Immature and Animals as Sexual Objects*

Whereas those sexual inverts whose sexual object does not belong to the normally adapted sex appear to the observer as a collective number of perhaps otherwise normal individuals, the persons who choose for their sexual object the sexually immature (children) are apparently from the first sporadic aberrations. Only exceptionally are children the exclusive sexual objects. They are mostly drawn into this rôle by a faint-hearted and impotent individual who makes use of such substitutes, or when an impulsive urgent desire cannot at the time secure the proper object. Still it throws some light on the nature of the sexual impulse, that it should suffer such great variation and depreciation of its object, a thing which hunger, adhering more energetically to its object, would allow only in the most extreme cases. The same may be said of sexual relations with animals—a thing not at all rare among farmers—where the sexual attraction goes beyond the limits of the species.

For esthetic reasons one would fain attribute this and other excessive aberrations of the sexual desire to the insane, but this cannot be done. Experience teaches that among the latter no disturbances of the sexual impulse can be found other than those observed among the sane, or among whole races and classes. Thus we find with gruesome frequency sexual abuse of children by teachers and servants merely because they have the best opportunities for it. The insane present the aforesaid aberration only in a somewhat intensified form; or what is of special significance is the fact that the aberration becomes exclusive and takes the place of the normal sexual gratification.

This very remarkable relation of sexual variations ranging from the normal to the insane gives material for reflection. It seems to me that the explanatory fact would show that the impulses of the sexual life belong to those which even normally are most poorly controlled by the higher psychic activities. He who is in any way psychically abnormal, be it in social or ethical conditions, is, according to my experience, regularly so in his sexual life. But many are abnormal in their sexual life who in every other respect correspond to the average; they have followed the human cultural development but sexuality remains as their weak point.

As a general result of these discussions we come to see that, under numerous conditions and among a surprising number of individuals, the nature and value of the sexual object steps into the background.   There is something else in the sexual impulse which is the essential and constant.[18]

2. DEVIATION IN REFERENCE TO THE SEXUAL AIM

The union of the genitals in the characteristic act of copulation is taken as the normal sexual aim.   It serves to loosen the sexual tension and temporarily to quench the sexual desire (gratification analogous to satiation of hunger).   Yet even in the most normal sexual process those additions are distinguishable, the development of which leads to the aberrations described as perversions. Thus certain intermediary relations to the sexual object connected with copulation, such as touching and looking, are recognized as preliminary to the sexual aim.   These activities are on the one hand themselves connected with pleasure and on the other hand they enhance the excitement which persists until the definite sexual aim is reached.   One definite kind of contiguity, consisting of mutual approximation of the mucous membranes of the lips in the form of a kiss, has among the most civilized nations received a sexual value, though the parts of the body concerned do not belong to the sexual apparatus but form the entrance to the digestive tract.   This therefore supplies the factors which allow us to bring the perversions into relation with the normal sexual life, and which are available also for their classification.   The perversions are either (a) anatomical transgressions of the bodily regions destined for the sexual union, or (b) a lingering at the intermediary relations to the sexual object which should normally be rapidly passed on the way to the definite sexual aim.

[18] The most pronounced difference between the sexual life (Liebesleben) of antiquity and ours lies in the fact that the ancients placed the emphasis on the impulse itself, while we put it on its object. The ancients extolled the impulse and were ready to ennoble through it even an inferior object, while we disparage the activity of the impulse as such and only countenance it on account of the merits of the object.

(a) Anatomical Transgression

Overestimation of the Sexual Object.—The psychic estimation in which the sexual object as a wish-aim of the sexual impulse participates, is only in the rarest cases limited to the genitals; generally it embraces the whole body and tends to include all sensations emanating from the sexual object. The same over-estimation spreads over the psychic sphere and manifests itself as a logical blinding (diminished judgment) in the face of the psychic attainments and perfections of the sexual object, as well as a blind obedience to the judgments issuing from the latter. The full faith of love thus becomes an important, if not the most primordial source of authority.[14]

It is this sexual over-valuation, which is at such variance with the limitation of the sexual aim to the union of the genitals only, that assists other parts of the body to participate as sexual aims. In the development of this most manifold anatomical over-estimation there is an unmistakable desire towards variation, a thing denominated by Hoche as " excitement-hunger " (Reizhunger).[15]

Sexual Utilization of the Mucous Membrane of the Lips and Mouth.—The significance of the factor of sexual over-estimation

[14] I must mention here that the blind obedience evinced by the hypnotized subject to the hypnotist causes me to think that the nature of hypnosis is to be found in the unconscious fixation of the libido on the person of the hypnotiser (by means of the masochistic component of the sexual impulse).

Ferenczi connects this character of suggestibility with the "parent complex " (Jahrbuch für Psychoanalytische und Psychopathologische Forschungen, I, 1909).

[15] Further investigations lead to the conclusion that I. Bloch has overestimated the factor of excitement-hunger (Reizhunger). The various roads upon which the libido moves behave to each other from the very beginning like communicating pipes; the factor of collateral streaming must also be considered.

can be best studied in the man, in whom alone the sexual life is accessible to investigation, whereas in the woman it is veiled in impenetrable darkness, partly in consequence of cultural stunting and partly on account of the conventional reticence and dishonesty of women.

The employment of the mouth as a sexual organ is considered as a perversion if the lips (tongue) of the one are brought into contact with the genitals of the other, but not when the mucous membrane of the lips of both touch each other. In the latter exception we find the connection with the normal. He who abhors the former as perversions, though these since antiquity have been common practices among mankind, yields to a distinct feeling of loathing which protects him from adopting such sexual aims. The limit of such loathing is frequently purely conventional; he who kisses fervently the lips of a pretty girl will perhaps be able to use her tooth brush only with a sense of loathing, though there is no reason to assume that his own oral cavity for which he entertains no loathing is cleaner than that of the girl. Our attention is here called to the factor of loathing which stands in the way of the libidinous over-estimation of the sexual aim, but which may in turn be vanquished by the libido. In the loathing we may observe one of the forces which have brought about the limitations of the sexual aim. As a rule these forces halt at the genitals; there is, however, no doubt that even the genitals of the other sex themselves may be an object of loathing. Such behavior is characteristic of all hysterics, especially women. The power of the sexual impulse by preference occupies itself with the overcoming of this loathing (see below).

Sexual Utilization of the Anal Opening.—It is even more obvious than in the former case that it is the loathing which stamps as a perversion the use of the anus as a sexual aim. But it should not be interpreted as espousing a cause when I observe that the basis of this loathing—namely, that this part of the body serves for the excretion and comes in contact with the loathsome excrement—if not more plausible than the basis which hysterical girls have for the disgust which they entertain for the male genital because it serves for urination.

The sexual rôle of the mucous membrane of the anus is by no means limited to intercourse between men; its preference has nothing characteristic of the inverted feeling. On the contrary, it seems that the pedicatio of the man owes its rôle to the analogy with the act in the woman, whereas among inverts it is mutual masturbation which is the most common sexual aim.

The **Significance of Other Parts of the Body.**—Sexual infringement on the other parts of the body, in all its variations, offers nothing new; it adds nothing to our knowledge of the sexual impulse which herein only announces its intention to occupy the sexual object in every way. Besides the sexual overvaluation, a second factor may be mentioned among the anatomical transgressions which is generally unknown. Certain parts of the body, like the mucous membrane of the mouth and anus, which repeatedly appear in such practices, lay claim as it were to be considered and treated as genitals. We shall hear how this claim is justified by the development of the sexual impulse, and how it is fulfilled in the symptomatology of certain morbid conditions.

Unfit Substitutes for the Sexual Object. Fetichism.—We are especially impressed by those cases in which for the normal sexual object is substituted another which is related to it but which is totally unfit for the normal sexual aim. According to the scheme of the introduction we should have done better to mention this most interesting group of aberrations of the sexual impulse among the deviations in reference to the sexual object, but we have deferred mention of these until we became acquainted with the factor of sexual over-estimation, upon which these manifestations, connected with the relinquishing of the sexual aim, depend.

The substitution for the sexual object is in general a part of the body but little adapted for sexual purposes, such as the foot, or hair, or an inanimate object which is in demonstrable relation with the sexual person, and mostly with the sexuality of the same (fragments of clothing, white underwear). This substitution is not unjustly compared with the fetich in which the savage sees the embodiment of his god.

The transition to the cases of fetichism, with a renunciation of the normal sexual aim or with a perverted sexual aim, is formed by cases in which a fetichistic determination is demanded in the sexual object if the sexual aim is to be attained (definite color of hair, clothing, even physical blemishes). No other variation of the sexual impulse verging on the pathological is so clear to us in every respect as this one, in spite of the peculiarity occasioned by its manifestations. A certain diminution in the striving for the normal sexual aim may be presupposed in all these cases (executive weakness of the sexual apparatus). The connection with the normal is occasioned by the psychologically necessary overestimation of the sexual object, which inevitably encroaches upon everything associatively related to it (sexual object). A certain degree of such fetichism therefore regularly belongs to the normal, especially during those stages of wooing when the normal sexual aim seems inaccessible or its realization deferred.

"Get me a handkerchief from her bosom—a garter of my love."
—Faust.

The case becomes pathological only when the striving for the fetich fixes itself beyond such determinations and takes the place of the normal sexual aim; or again, when the fetich disengages itself from the person concerned and itself becomes a sexual object. These are the general determinations for the transition of mere variations of the sexual impulse into pathological aberrations.

The persistent influence of a sexual impress mostly received in early childhood often shows itself in the selection of a fetich, as Binet first asserted, and as was later proven by many illustrations,—a thing which may be placed parallel to the proverbial attachment to a first love in the normal ("On revient toujours à ses premiers amours"). Such a connection is especially seen in cases with only fetichistic determinations of the sexual object. The significance of early sexual impressions will be met again in other places.

In other cases it was mostly a symbolic thought association, unconscious to the person concerned, which led to the substitution of the object by means of a fetich. The paths of these connections can not always be definitely demonstrated. The foot is a very primitive sexual symbol already found in myths.[16] Fur is used as a fetich probably on account of its association with the hairiness of the mons veneris. Such symbolism seems often to depend on sexual experiences in childhood.[17]

(b) Fixation of Precursory Sexual Aims

The Appearance of Newer Intentions.—All the outer and inner determinations which impede or hold at a distance the attainment of the normal sexual aim, such as impotence, costliness of the sexual object, and dangers of the sexual act, will con-

---

[16] The shoe or slipper is accordingly a symbol for the female genital.

[17] Psychoanalysis has filled up the gap in the understanding of fetichisms by showing that the selection of the fetich depends on a coprophilic smell-desire which has been lost by repression. Feet and hair are strong smelling objects which are raised to fetiches after the renouncing of the now unpleasant sensation of smell. Accordingly, only the filthy and ill-smelling foot is the sexual object in the perversion which corresponds to the foot fetichism. Another contribution to the explanation of the fetichistic preference of the foot is found in the Infantile Sexual Theories (see later). The foot replaces the penis which is so much missed in the woman.

ceivably strengthen the inclination to linger at the preparatory acts and to form them into new sexual aims which may take the place of the normal. On closer investigation it is always seen that the ostensibly most peculiar of these new intentions have already been indicated in the normal sexual act.

Touching and Looking.—At least a certain amount of touching is indispensable for a person in order to attain the normal sexual aim. It is also generally known that the touching of the skin of the sexual object causes much pleasure and produces a supply of new excitement. Hence, the lingering at the touching can hardly be considered a perversion if the sexual act is proceeded with.

The same holds true with looking which is analogous to touching. The manner in which the libidinous excitement is frequently awakened is by the optical impression, and selection takes account of this circumstance by making the sexual object a thing of beauty. The covering of the body, which keeps abreast with civilization, serves to arouse sexual inquisitiveness, which always strives to restore for itself the sexual object by uncovering the hidden parts. This can be turned into the artistic ("sublimation") if the interest is turned from the genitals to the form of the body. The tendency to linger at this intermediary sexual aim of the sexually accentuated looking is found to a certain degree in most normals; indeed it gives them the possibility of directing a certain amount of their libido to a higher artistic aim. On the other hand, the fondness for looking becomes a perversion (a) when it limits itself entirely to the genitals; (b) when it becomes connected with the overcoming of loathing (voyeurs and onlookers at the functions of excretion); and (c) when instead of preparing for the normal sexual aim it suppresses it. The latter, if I may draw conclusions from a single analysis, is in a most pronounced way true of exhibitionists, who expose their genitals so as in turn to bring to view the genitals of others.

In the perversion which consists in striving to look and be

looked at we are confronted with a very remarkable character which will occupy us even more intensively in the following aberration. The sexual aim is here present in twofold formation, in an active and a passive form.

The force which is opposed to the peeping mania and through which it is eventually abolished is shame (like the former loathing).

Sadism and Masochism.—The desire to cause pain to the sexual object and its opposite, the most frequent and most significant of all perversions, was designated in its two forms by v. Krafft-Ebing as sadism or the active form, and masochism or the passive form. Other authors prefer the narrower term algolagnia which emphasizes the pleasure in pain and cruelty, whereas the terms selected by v. Krafft-Ebing place the pleasure secured in all kinds of humility and submission in the foreground.

The roots of active algolagnia, sadism, can be readily demonstrahle in the normal. The sexuality of most men shows a taint of aggression, it is a propensity to subdue, the biological significance of which lies in the necessity of overcoming the resistance of the sexual object by actions other than mere courting. Sadism would then correspond to an aggressive component of the sexual impulse which has become independent and exaggerated and has been brought to the foreground by displacement.

The origin of at least one of the roots of masochism is just as certain. It originates from the sexual over-estimation as a necessary psychic sequence of the selection of a sexual object. The pain which is here overcome ranks with the loathing and shame which were the resistances opposed to the libido.

That cruelty and sexual impulse are most intimately connected is beyond doubt taught by the history of civilization, but in the explanation of this connection no one has gone beyond the accentuation of the aggressive factors of the libido. The aggression which is mixed with the sexual impulse is according to some authors a remnant of cannibalistic lust, a participation on the part of the acquisition apparatus (Bemächtigungsapparatus) which served also for the gratification of the great wants of the other, ontogenetically the older impulse. It has also been claimed that every pain contains in itself the possibility of a pleasurable sensation. Let us be satisfied with the impression that the explanation of this perversion is by no means satisfactory and that it is possible that many psychic efforts unite themselves into one effect.

The most striking peculiarity of this perversion lies in the fact that its active and passive forms are regularly encountered together in the same person. He who experiences pleasure by causing pain to others in sexual relations is also able to experience the pain emanating from sexual relations as pleasure. A sadist is simultaneously a masochist, though either the active or the passive side of the perversion may be more strongly developed and thus represent his preponderate sexual activity.[18]

We thus see that certain perverted propensities regularly appear in contrasting pairs, a thing which, in view of the material to be produced later, must claim great theoretical value. It is furthermore clear that the existence of the contrast, sadism and masochism, can not readily be attributed to the mixture of aggression. On the other hand it may be attempted to connect such simultaneously existing contrasts with the united contrast of male and female in bisexuality.

3. General Statements Applicable to all Perversions

Variation and Disease.—The physicians who at first studied the perversions in pronounced cases and under peculiar conditions were naturally inclined to attribute to them the character of a morbid or degenerative sign similar to the inversions. This

[18] Instead of substantiating this statement by many examples I will merely cite Havelock Ellis (The Sexual Impulse, 1903) : " All known cases of sadism and masochism, even those cited by v. Krafft-Ebing, always show (as has already been shown by Colin, Scott, and Féré) traces of both groups of manifestations in the same individual."

view, however, is easier to refute in this than in the former case. Everyday experience has shown that most of these transgressions, at least the milder ones, are seldom wanting as components in the sexual life of normals who look upon them as upon other intimacies. Wherever the conditions are favorable such a perversion may for a long time be substituted by a normal person for the normal sexual aim or it may be placed near it. In no normal person does the normal sexual aim lack some designable perverse element, and this universality suffices in itself to prove the inexpediency of an opprobrious application of the name perversion. In the realm of the sexual life one is sure to meet with exceptional difficulties which are at present really unsolvable, if one wishes to draw a sharp line between the mere variations within physiological limits and morbid symptoms.

Nevertheless, the quality of the new sexual aim in some of these perversions is such as to require special notice. Some of the perversions are in content so distant from the normal that we cannot help calling them "morbid," especially those in which the sexual impulse, in overcoming the resistances (shame, loathing, fear, and pain) has brought about surprising results (licking of feces and violation of cadavers). Yet even in these cases one ought not to feel certain of regularly finding among the perpetrators persons of pronounced abnormalities or insane minds. We can not lose sight of the fact that persons who otherwise behave normally are recorded as sick in the realm of the sexual life where they are dominated by the most unbridled of all impulses. On the other hand, a manifest abnormality in any other relation in life generally shows an undercurrent of abnormal sexual behavior.

In the majority of cases we are able to find the morbid character of the perversion not in the content of the new sexual aim but in its relation to the normal. It is morbid if the perversion does not appear beside the normal (sexual aim and sexual object), where favorable circumstances promote it and unfavorable impede the normal, or if it has under all circumstances repressed and supplanted the normal; the exclusiveness and fixation of the perversion justifies us in considering it a morbid symptom.

The Psychic Participation in the Perversions.—Perhaps even in the most abominable perversions we must recognize the most prolific psychic participation for the transformation of the sexual impulse. In these cases a piece of psychic work has been accomplished in which, in spite of its gruesome success, the value of an idealization of the impulse can not be disputed. The omnipotence of love nowhere perhaps shows itself stronger than in this one of her aberrations. The highest and the lowest everywhere in sexuality hang most intimately together. ("From heaven through the world to hell.")

Two Results.—In the study of perversions we have gained an insight into the fact that the sexual impulse has to struggle against certain psychic forces, resistances, among which shame and loathing are most prominent. We may presume that these forces are employed to confine the impulse within the accepted normal limits, and if they have become developed in the individual before the sexual impulse has attained its full strength, it is really they which have directed in the course of development.

We have furthermore remarked that some of the examined perversions can be comprehended only by assuming the union of many motives. If they are amenable to analysis—disintegrattion—they must be of a composite nature. This may give us a hint that the sexual impulse itself may not be something simple, that it may on the contrary be composed of many components which detach themselves to form perversions. Our clinical observation thus calls our attention to fusions which have iis feited their expression in the uniform normal behavior.

4. THE SEXUAL IMPULSE IN NEUROTICS

Psychoanalysis.—A proper contribution to the knowledge the sexual impulse in persons who are at least related to normal can be gained only from one source, and is accessible only by one definite path. There is only one way to obtain a thorough and unerring solution of problems in the sexual life of so-called psychoneurotics (hysteria, obsessions, the wrongly-named neurasthenia, and probably also paranoia), and that is by subjecting them to the psychoanalytic investigations propounded by J. Breuer and myself in 1893, which we called the "cathartic" treatment.

I must repeat what I have said in my published work, that these psychoneuroses, as far as my experience goes, are based on sexual motive powers. I do not mean that the energy of the sexual impulse contributes to the forces supporting the morbid manifestations (symptoms), but I wish distinctly to maintain that this supplies the only constant and the most important source of energy in the neurosis, so that the sexual life of such persons manifests itself either exclusively, preponderately, or partially in these symptoms. As I have already stated in different places, the symptoms are the sexual activities of the patient. The proof for this assertion I have obtained from the psychoanalysis of hysterics and other neurotics during a period of fifteen years, the results of which I hope to give later in a detailed account.

The psychoanalysis removes the symptoms of hysteria on the supposition that they are the substitutes—the transcriptions as it were—for a series of emotionally accentuated psychic processes, wishes, and desires, to which a passage for their discharge through the conscious psychic activities has been cut off by a special process (repression). These thought formations which are restrained in the state of the unconscious strive for expression, that is, for discharge, in conformity to their affective value, and find such in hysteria through a process of conversion into somatic phenomena—the hysterical symptoms. If, *lege artis,* and with the aid of a special technique, retrogressive transformations of the symptoms into the affectful and conscious thoughts can be affected, it then becomes possible to get the most accurate infor-

mation about the nature and origin of these previously unconscious psychic formations.

Results of Psychoanalysis.—In this manner it has been discovered that the symptoms represent the equivalent for the strivings which received their strength from the source of the sexual
impulse. This fully concurs with what we know of the character of hysterics, which we have taken as models for all psychoneurotics, before it has become diseased, and with what we know
concerning the causes of the disease. The hysterical character
evinces a part of sexual repression which reaches beyond the
normal limits, an exaggeration of the resistances against the
sexual impulse which we know as shame and loathing. It is an
instinctive flight from intellectual occupation with the sexual
problem, the consequence of which in pronounced cases is a complete sexual ignorance, which is preserved till the age of sexual
maturity is attained.[19]

This feature so characteristic of hysteria is not seldom con-
cealed in crude observation by the existence of the second constitutional factor of hysteria, namely, the enormous development
of the sexual craving. But the psychological analysis will always
reveal it and solves the very contradictory enigma of hysteria by
proving the existence of the contrasting pair, an immense sexual
desire and a very exaggerated sexual rejection.

The provocation of the disease in hysterically predisposed persons is brought about if in consequence of their progressive
maturity or external conditions of life they are earnestly confronted with the real sexual demand. Between the pressure of
the craving and the opposition of the sexual rejection an outlet
for the disease results, which does not remove the conflict but
seeks to elude it by transforming the libidinous strivings into

---

[19] Studien über Hysterie, 1895, J. Breuer tells of the patient on whom
he first practiced the cathartic method: "The sexual moment was sur-
prisingly undeveloped."

symptoms. It is an exception only in appearance if a hysterical person, say a man, becomes subject to some banal emotional disturbance, to a conflict in the center of which there is no sexual interest. The psychoanalysis will regularly show that it is the sexual components of the conflict which make the disease possible by withdrawing the psychic processes from normal adjustment.

Neurosis and Perversion.—A great part of the opposition to my assertion is explained by the fact that the sexuality from which I deduce the psychoneurotic symptoms is thought of as coincident with the normal sexual impulse. But the psychoanalysis teaches us better than this. It shows that the symptoms do not by any means result at the expense only of the so called normal sexual impulse (at least not exclusively or preponderately), but they represent the converted expression of impulses which in a broader sense might be designated as perverse if they could manifest themselves directly in phantasies and acts without deviating from consciousness. The symptoms are therefore partially formed at the cost of abnormal sexuality. The neurosis is, so to say, the negative of the perversion.[20]

The sexual impulse of the psychoneurotic shows all the aberrations which we have studied as variations of the normal and as manifestations of morbid sexual life.

(*a*) In all the neurotics without exception we find feelings of inversion in the unconscious psychic life, fixation of libido on persons of the same sex. It is impossible, without a deep and searching discussion, adequately to appreciate the significance of this factor for the formation of the picture of the disease; I can only assert that the unconscious propensity to inversion is never

[20] The well-known fancies of perverts which under favorable conditions are changed into contrivances, the delusional fears of paranoiacs which are in a hostile manner projected on others, and the unconscious fancies of hysterics which are discovered in their symptoms by psychoanalysis, agree as to content in the minutest details.

wanting and is particularly of immense service in explaining male hysteria.[21]

(*b*) All the inclinations to anatomical transgression can be demonstrated in psychoneurotics in the unconscious and as symptom-creators. Of special frequency and intensity are those which impart to the mouth and the mucous membrane of the anus the rôle of genitals.

(*c*) The partial desires which usually appear in contrasting pairs play a very prominent rôle among the symptom-creators in the psychoneuroses. We have learned to know them as carriers of new sexual aims, such as peeping mania, exhibitionism, and the actively and passively formed impulses of cruelty. The contribution of the last is indispensable for the understanding of the morbid nature of the symptoms; it almost regularly controls some portion of the social behavior of the patient. The transformation of love into hatred, of tenderness into hostility, which is characteristic of a large number of neurotic cases and apparently of all cases of paranoia, takes place by means of the union of cruelty with the libido.

The interest in these deductions is heightened on account of certain peculiar circumstances, as follows:

α. There is nothing in the unconscious streams of thought in the neuroses which would correspond to an inclination towards fetichism; a circumstance which throws light on the psychological peculiarity of this well understood perversion.

β. Wherever any such impulse is found in the unconscious which can be paired with a contrasting one, it can regularly be demonstrated that the latter, too, is effective. Every active per-

---

[21] A psychoneurosis very often associates itself with a manifest inversion in which the heterosexual feeling becomes subjected to complete repression.—It is but just to state that the necessity of a general recognition of the tendency to inversion in psychoneurotics was first imparted to me personally by Wilh. Fliess, of Berlin, after I had myself discovered it in some cases.

version is here accompanied by its passive opponent. He who in the unconscious is an exhibitionist is at the same time a voyeur, he who suffers from sadistic feelings as a result of repression will also show another reinforcement of the symptoms from the source of masochistic tendencies. The perfect concurrence with the behavior of the corresponding positive perversions is certainly very noteworthy. In the picture of the disease, however, the preponderant rôle is played by either one or the other of the opposing tendencies.

γ. In a pronounced case of psychoneurosis we seldom find the development of one single perverted impulse; usually there are many and regularly there are traces of all perversions. The individual impulse, however, on account of its intensity, is independent of the development of the others, but the study of the positive perversions gives us the accurate opponent to it.

PARTIAL IMPULSES AND EROGENOUS ZONES

Keeping in mind what we have learned from the examination of the positive and negative perversions, it becomes quite obvious that they can be referred to a number of "partial impulses," which are not, however, primary but are subject to further analysis. In a non-sexual "impulse" originating from impulses of motor sources we can distinguish a contribution from a stimulus-receiving organ, such as the skin, mucous membrane, and sensory organs. This we shall here designate as an erogenous zone; it is that organ the stimulus of which bestows on the impulse the sexual character. In the perversions which claim sexual significance for the oral cavity and the anal opening the part played by the erogenous zone is quite obvious. It behaves in every way ' like a part of the sexual apparatus. In hysteria these parts of the body, as well as their tracks of mucous membrane, become the seat of new sensations and innervating changes in a manner similar to the real genitals when under the excitement of normal sexual processes.

The significance of the erogenous zones in the psychoneuroses, as additional apparatus and substitutes for the genitals, appears to be most prominent in hysteria though that does not signify that it is of lesser validity in the other morbid forms. It is not so recognizable in compulsion neurosis and paranoia because here the symptom formation takes place in regions of the psychic apparatus which lie at a great distance from the central locations for bodily control. The more remarkable thing in the compulsion neurosis is the significance of the impulses which create new sexual aims and appear independently of the erogenous zones. Nevertheless, the eye corresponds to an erogenous zone in the looking and exhibition mania, while the skin takes on the same part in the pain and cruelty components of the sexual impulse. The skin, which in special parts of the body becomes differentiated as sensory organs and modified by the mucous membrane, is the erogenous zone, κατ'εξοχήν.[22]

Explanation of the Manifest Preponderance of Sexual Perversions in the Psychoneuroses

The sexuality of psychoneurotics has perhaps been placed in a false light by the above discussions. It appears that the sexual behavior of the psychoneurotic approaches in predisposition to the pervert and deviates by just so much from the normal. Nevertheless, it is very possible that the constitutional disposition of these patients besides containing an immense amount of sexual repression and a predominant force of sexual impulse also possesses an unusual tendency to perversions in the broadest sense. However, an examination of milder cases shows that the last assumption is not an absolute requisite, or at least that in pro-

---

[22] One should here think of Moll's assertion, who divides the sexual impulse into the impulses of contrectation and detumescence. Contrectation signifies a desire to touch the skin. In one of his cases Strohmayer has very correctly found the origin of obsessive reproaches in suppressed sadistic feelings.

nouncing judgment on the morbid effects one ought to discount the effect of this latter factor. In most psychoneurotics the disease first appears after puberty following the demands of the normal sexual life, but against this the repression directs itself. Or the disease comes on later, owing to the fact that the libido is unable to attain normal sexual gratification. In both cases the libido behaves like a stream the principal bed of which is dammed; it fills the collateral roads which until now perhaps have been empty. Thus the manifestly great (though to be sure negative) tendency to perversion in psychoneurotics may be collaterally conditioned; at any rate, it is certainly collaterally increased. The fact of the matter is that the sexual repression has to be added as an inner moment to such external ones as limitation of freedom, inaccessibility to the normal sexual object, dangers of the normal sexual act, etc., which cause the origin of perversions in individuals who might have otherwise remained normal.

In individual cases of neurosis the behavior may be different; now the congenital force of the tendency to perversion may be more decisive and at other times more influence may be exerted by the collateral increase of the same through the deviation of the libido from the normal sexual aim and object. It would be unjust to construe a contrast where a coöperation exists. The greatest effect will always be brought about in a neurosis if there is a collaboration of constitution and experience working in the same direction. A pronounced constitution may perhaps be able to dispense with the assistance of impressions, while a profound disturbance in life may perhaps bring on a neurosis even in an average constitution. These views similarly hold true in the etiological significance of the congenital and the accidental experiences in other spheres.

If, however, preference is given to the assumption that an especially formed tendency to perversions is characteristic of the psychoneurotic constitution, there is a prospect of being able to distinguish a multiformity of such constitutions in accordance with the congenital preponderance of this or that erogenous zone, or of this or that partial impulse. Whether there is a special relationship between the perverted predisposition and the selection of the morbid picture has not, like many other things in this realm, been investigated.

REFERENCE TO THE INFANTILISM OF SEXUALITY

By demonstrating the perverted feelings as symptomatic formations in psychoneurotics, we have enormously increased the number of persons who can be added to the perverts. This is not only because neurotics represent a very large proportion of humanity, but we must consider also that the neuroses in all their gradations run in an uninterrupted series to the normal state. Moebius was quite justified in saying that we are all somewhat hysterical. Hence, the very wide dissemination of perversions urged us to assume that the predisposition to perversions is no rare peculiarity but must form a part of the normally accepted constitution.

We have heard that it is a question whether perversions should be referred to congenital determinations or whether they originate from accidental experiences, just as Binet showed in fetichisms. Now we are confronted with the conclusion that there is indeed something congenital at the basis of perversions, but it is something which is congenital in all persons, which as a predisposition may fluctuate in intensity and is brought into prominence by influences of life. We deal here with congenital roots in the constitution of the sexual impulse which in one series of cases develop into real carriers of sexual activity (perverts); while in other cases they undergo an insufficient suppression (repression), so that as morbid symptoms they are enabled to attract to themselves in a round-about way a considerable part of the sexual energy; while again in favorable cases between the two extremes they cause the origin of the normal sexual life through effective limitations and other elaborations.

But we must also remember that the assumed constitution which shows the roots of all perversions will be demonstrable only in the child, though all impulses can be manifested in it only in moderate intensity. If we are led to suppose that neurotics conserve the infantile state of their sexuality or return to it, our interest must then turn to the sexual life of the child, and we will then follow the play of influences which control the processes of development of the infantile sexuality up to its termination in a perversion, a neurosis, or a normal sexual life.

II

THE INFANTILE SEXUALITY

It is a part of popular belief about the sexual impulse that it is absent in childhood and that it first appears in the period of life known as puberty. This, though an obvious error, is a serious one in its consequences and is chiefly due to our present ignorance of the fundamental principles of the sexual life. A comprehensive study of the sexual manifestations of childhood would probably reveal to us the existence of the essential features of the sexual impulse, and would make us acquainted with its development and its composition from various sources.

The Neglect of the Infantile.—It is remarkable that those writers who endeavor to explain the qualities and reactions of the adult individual have given so much more attention to the ancestral period than to the period of the individual's own existence—that is, they have attributed more influence to heredity than to childhood. As a matter of fact, it might well be supposed that the influence of the latter period would be easier to understand, and that it would be entitled to more consideration than heredity. To be sure, one occasionally finds in medical literature notes on the premature sexual activities of small children, about erections and masturbation and even actions resembling coitus, but these are referred to merely as exceptional occurrences, as curiosities, or as deterring examples of premature perversity. No author has to my knowledge recognized the lawfulness of the sexual impulse in childhood, and in the numerous writings on the development of the child the chapter on "Sexual Development" is usually passed over.[1]

[1] This assertion on revision seemed even to myself so bold that I decided to test its correctness by again reviewing the literature. The result

34

Infantile Amnesia.—This remarkable negligence is due partly to conventional considerations, which influence the writers on account of their own bringing up, and partly to a psychic phenomenon which has thus far remained unexplained. I refer to

of this second review did not warrant any change in my original statement. The scientific elaboration of the physical as well as the psychic phenomena of the infantile sexuality is still in its initial stages. One author (S. Bell, "A Preliminary Study of the Emotions of Love Between the Sexes," American Journal of Psychology, XIII, 1902) says: "I know of no scientist who has given a careful analysis of the emotion as it is seen in the adolescent." The only attention given to somatic sexual manifestations occurring before the age of puberty was in connection with degenerative manifestations, and these were referred to as a sign of degeneration. A chapter on the sexual life of children is not to be found in all the representative psychologies of this age which I have read. Among these works I can mention the following: Preyer; Baldwin (The Development of the Mind in the Child and in the Race, 1898); Pérez (L'enfant de 3-7 ans, 1894); Strümpel (Die pädagogische Pathologie, 1899); Karl Groos (Das Seelenleben des Kindes, 1904); Th. Heller (Grundriss der Heilpädagogic, 1904); Sully (Observations Concerning Childhood, 1897). The best impression of the present situation of this sphere can be obtained from the journal Die Kinderfehler (issued since 1896). On the other hand one gains the impression that the existence of love in childhood is in no need of demonstration. Pérez (l. c.) speaks for it; K. Groos (Die Spiele der Menschen, 1899) states that some children are very early subject to sexual emotions, and show a desire to touch the other sex (p. 336); S. Bell observed the earliest appearance of sex-love in a child during the middle part of its third year. See also Havelock Ellis, The Sexual Impulse, Appendix II.

The above-mentioned judgment concerning the literature of infantile sexuality no longer holds true since the appearance of the great and important work of G. Stanley Hall (Adolescence, Its Psychology and its Relation to Physiology, Anthropology, Sociology, Sex, Crime, Religion, and Education, 2 vols., New York, 1908). The recent book of A. Moll, Das Sexualleben des Kindes, Berlin, 1909, offers no occasion for such a modification. See, on the other hand, Bleuler, Sexuelle abnormitäten der Kinder (Jahrbuch der Schweizerischen Gesellschaft für Schulgesundheitspflege, IX, 1908).

the peculiar amnesia which veils from most people (not from all!) the first years of their childhood, usually the first six or eight years. So far it has not occurred to us that this amnesia ought to surprise us, though we have in fact good reasons for surprise. For we are informed that in those years from which we later obtain nothing except a few incomprehensible memory fragments, we have vividly reacted to impressions, that we have manifested pain and pleasure like any human being, that we have evinced love, jealousy, and other passions as they then affected us; indeed we are told that we have uttered remarks which proved to grown-ups that we possessed understanding and a budding power of judgment. Still we know nothing of all this when we become older. Why does our memory lag behind all our other psychic activities? We really have reason to believe that at no time of life are we more capable of impressions and reproductions than during the years of childhood.[2]

On the other hand we must assume, or we may convince ourselves through psychological observations on others, that the very impressions which we have forgotten have nevertheless left the deepest traces in our psychic life, and acted as determinants for our whole future development. We conclude therefore that we do not deal with a real forgetting of infantile impressions but rather with an amnesia similar to that observed in neurotics for later experiences, the nature of which consists in their being detained from consciousness (repression). But what forces bring about this repression of the infantile impressions? He who can solve this riddle will also explain hysterical amnesia.

We shall not, however, hesitate to assert that the existence of the infantile amnesia gives us a new point of comparison between the psychic states of the child and those of the psychoneurotic. We have already encountered another point of com-

[2] I have attempted to solve the problems presented by the earliest infantile recollections in a paper, " Über Deckerinnerungen " 'Monatsschrift für Psychiatrie und Neurologie, VI, 1899).

parison when confronted by the fact that the sexuality of the psychoneurotic preserves the infantile character or has returned to it. May there not be an ultimate connection between the infantile and the hysterical amnesias?

The connection between the infantile and the hysterical amnesias is really more than a mere play of wit. The hysterical amnesia which serves the repression can only be explained by the fact that the individual already possesses a sum of recollections which have been withdrawn from conscious disposal and which by associative connection now seize that which is acted upon by the repelling forces of the repression emanating from consciousness. We may say that without infantile amnesia there would be no hysterical amnesia.

I believe that the infantile amnesia which causes the individual to look upon his childhood as if it were a prehistoric time and conceals from him the beginning of his own sexual life—that this amnesia is responsible for the fact that one does not usually attribute any value to the infantile period in the development of the sexual life. One single observer cannot fill the gap which has been thus produced in our knowledge. As early as 1896 I had already emphasized the significance of childhood for the origin of certain important phenomena connected with the sexual life, and since then I have not ceased to put into the foreground the importance of the infantile factor for sexuality.

The Sexual Latency Period of Childhood and its Emergence

The extraordinary frequent discoveries of apparently abnormal and exceptional sexual manifestations in childhood, as well as the discovery of infantile reminiscences in neurotics, which were hitherto unconscious, allow us to sketch the following picture of the sexual behavior of childhood.[3]

[3] The use of the latter material is justified by the fact that the age of childhood of those who are later neurotics need not necessarily differ from that of those who are later normal.

It seems certain that the newborn child brings with it the germs of sexual feelings which continue to develop for some time and then succumb to a progressive suppression, which is in turn broken through by the proper advances of the sexual development and which can be checked by individual idiosyncrasies. Nothing definite is known concerning the lawfulness and periodicity of this oscillating course of development. It seems, however, that the sexual life of the child mostly manifests itself in the third or fourth year in some form accessible to observation.[4]

The Sexual Inhibition.—It is during this period of total or at least partial latency that the psychic forces develop which later act as inhibitions on the sexual life, and narrow its direction like dams. These psychic forces are loathing, shame, and moral and esthetic ideation masses. We may gain the impression that the erection of these dams in the civilized child is the work of education; and surely education contributes much to it. In reality, however, this development is organically determined and can occasionally be produced without the help of education. Indeed education remains properly within its assigned realm only if it strictly follows the path sketched for it by the organic determinant and impresses it somewhat cleaner and deeper.

Reaction Formation and Sublimation.—What are the means that accomplish these very important constructions so significant for the later personal culture and normality? They are probably brought about at the cost of the infantile sexuality itself, the influx of which has not stopped even in this latency period—

[4] An anatomic analogy to the behavior of the infantile sexual function formulated by me is perhaps given by Bayer (Deutsches Archiv für klin. ische Medizin, Bd. 73) who claims that the internal genitals (uterus) are regularly larger in newborn than in older children. However Halban's conception, that after birth there is also an involution of the other parts of the sexual apparatus, has not been verified. According to Halban (Zeitschrift für Geburtshilfe u. Gynäkologie, LIII, 1904) this process of involution ends after a few weeks of extra-uterine life.

the energy of which indeed has been turned away either wholly or partially from sexual utilization and conducted to other aims. The historians of civilization seem to be unanimous in the opinion that such deviation of sexual motive powers from sexual aims to new aims, a process which merits the name of *sublimation,* has furnished powerful components for all cultural accomplishments. We will therefore add that the same process acts in the development of every individual, and that it begins to act in the sexual latency period.[5]

We can also venture an opinion about the mechanisms of such sublimation. The sexual feelings of these infantile years on the one hand could not be utilizable, since the procreating functions are postponed,—this is the chief character of the latency period; on the other hand, they would in themselves be perverse, as they would emanate from erogenous zones and would be born of impulses which in the individual's course of development could only evoke a feeling of displeasure. They therefore awaken contrary forces (feelings of reaction), which in order to suppress such displeasure, build up the above mentioned psychic dams: loathing, shame, and morality.

The Emergence of the Latency Period.—Without deluding ourselves as to the hypothetical nature and deficient clearness of our understanding regarding the infantile period of latency and delay, we will return to reality and state that such a' utilization of the infantile sexuality represents an ideal bringing up from which the development of the individual usually deviates in some measure and often very considerably. A portion of the sexual manifestation 'occasionally breaks through which has withdrawn from sublimation, or a sexual activity remains throughout the whole duration of the latency period until the reinforced breaking through of the sexual impulse in puberty. In so far as they have paid any attention to infantile sexuality the educators behave as

[5] The expression "sexual latency period" (sexuelle latenz-periode") I have borrowed from W. Fliess.

4

if they shared our views concerning the formation of the moral forces of defence at the cost of sexuality, and as if they knew that sexual activity makes the child uneducable; for the educators consider all sexual manifestations of the child as an " evil " in the face of which little can be accomplished. We have, however, every reason for directing our attention to those phenomena so much feared by the educators, for we expect to find in them the solution of the primitive formation of the sexual impulse.

The Manifestations of the Infantile Sexuality

For reasons which we shall discuss later we will take as a model of the infantile sexual manifestations thumbsucking (pleasure-sucking), to which the Hungarian pediatrist, Lindner, has devoted an excellent essay.[6]

Thumbsucking.—Thumbsucking, which manifests itself in the nursing baby and which may be continued till maturity or throughout life, consists in a rhythmic repetition of sucking contact with the mouth (the lips), wherein the purpose of taking nourishment is excluded. A part of the lip itself, the tongue, which is another preferable skin region within reach, and even the big toe—may be taken as objects for sucking. Simultaneously, there is also a desire to grasp things, which manifests itself in a rhythmical pulling of the ear lobe and which may cause the child to grasp a part of another person (generally the ear) for the same purpose. The pleasure-sucking is connected with an entire exhaustion of attention and leads to sleep or even to a motor reaction in the form of an orgasm.[7] Pleasure-sucking is often combined with a rubbing contact with certain sensitive parts of the body, such as the breast and external genitals. It is by this road that many children go from thumb-sucking to masturbation.

[6] Jahrbuch für Kinderheilkunde, N. F., XIV, 1879.

[7] This already shows what holds true for the whole life, namely that sexual gratification is the best hypnotic. Most nervous insomnias are traced to lack of sexual gratification. It is also known that unscrupulous nurses calm crying children to sleep by stroking their genitals.

No investigator has yet doubted the sexual nature of this action.[8] Still, the best theories based on the observations of adults leave us in the lurch in the face of this manifestation of infantile sexual activity. If we think of Moll's division of the sexual impulse, the detumescence and contrection impulses, we find that the first factor is here out of question, and that the second can be recognized only with difficulty, as Moll later apparently describes this also as a detumescence impulse directed against other persons.

Autoerotism.—It is our duty here to arrange this state of affairs differently. Let us insist that the most striking character of this sexual activity is that the impulse is not directed against other persons but that it gratifies itself on its own body; to use the happy term invented by Havelock Ellis, we will say that it is autoerotic.[9]

It is, moreover, clear that the action of the thumbsucking child is determined by the fact that it seeks a pleasure which has already been experienced and is now remembered. Through the rhythmic sucking on a portion of the skin or mucous membrane it finds the gratification in the simplest way. It is also easy to conjecture on what occasions the child first experienced this pleasure which it now strives to renew. The first and most important activity in the child's life, the sucking from the mother's breast (or its substitute), must have acquainted it with this pleasure. We would say that the child's lips behaved like an erogenous zone, and that the excitement through the warm stream of milk was really the cause of the pleasurable sensation. To be sure, the gratification of the erogenous zone was at first united with the gratification of taking nourishment. He who sees a satiated child sink back from the mother's breast, and merge into sleep with

[8] A recent exception is Moll (Das Sexualleben des Kindes).
[9] Ellis spoils, however, the sense of his invented term by comprising under the phenomena of autoerotism the whole of hysteria and masturbation in its full extent.

reddened cheeks and blissful smile, will have to admit that this picture remains as a guide for the expression of sexual gratification in later life. But the desire for repetition of the sexual gratification is separated from the desire for taking nourishment; a separation which becomes unavoidable with the appearance of the teeth when the nourishment is no longer sucked in but chewed. The child does not make use of a strange object for sucking but prefers its own skin because it is more convenient, because it thus makes itself independent of the outer world which it cannot yet control, and because in this way it creates for itself, as it were, a second, even if an inferior, erogenous zone. The inferiority of this second region urges it later to seek the same parts, the lips of another person. ("It is a pity that I cannot kiss myself," might be attributed to it.)

Not all children suck their thumbs. It may be assumed that it is found only in children in whom the erogenous significance of the lip-zone is constitutionally reënforced. Children in whom this is retained are habitual kissers as adults and show a tendency to perverse kissing, or as men they have a marked desire for drinking and smoking. But if repression comes into play they experience disgust for eating and evince hysterical vomiting. By virtue of the community of the lip-zone the repression encroaches upon the impulse of nourishment. Many of my female patients showing disturbances in eating, such as hysterical globus, choking sensations, and vomiting, have been energetic thumbsuckers during infancy.

In the thumbsucking or pleasure-sucking we have already been able to observe the two essential characters of one infantile sexual manifestation. This manifestation does not yet know any sexual object, it is autoerotic and its sexual aim is under the control of an erogenous zone. Let us assume for the present that these characters also hold true for most of the other activities of the infantile sexual impulse.

THE SEXUAL AIM OF THE INFANTILE SEXUALITY

The Characters of the Erogenous Zones.—From the example of thumbsucking we may gather a great many points useful for the distinguishing of an erogenous zone. It is a portion of skin or mucous membrane in which the stimuli produce a feeling of pleasure of definite quality. There is no doubt that the pleasure-producing stimuli are governed by special determinants which we do not know. The rhythmic characters must play some part in them and this strongly suggests an analogy to tickling. It does not, however, appear so certain whether the character of the pleasurable feeling evoked by the stimulus can be designated as "peculiar," and in what part of this peculiarity the sexual factor exists. Psychology is still groping in the dark when it concerns matters of pleasure and pain, and the most cautious assumption is therefore the most advisable. We may perhaps later come upon reasons which seem to support the peculiar quality of the sensation of pleasure.

The erogenous quality may adhere most notably to definite regions of the body. As is shown by the example of thumbsucking, there are predestined erogenous zones. But the same example also shows that any other region of skin or mucous membrane may assume the function of an erogenous zone; it must therefore carry along a certain adaptability. The production of the sensation of pleasure therefore depends more on the quality of the stimulus than on the nature of the bodily region. The thumbsucking child looks around on his body and selects any portion of it for pleasure-sucking, and becoming accustomed to it, he then prefers it. If he accidentally strikes upon a predestined region, such as breast, nipple or genitals, it naturally has the preference. A quite analogous tendency to displacement is again found in the symptomatology of hysteria. In this neurosis the repression mostly concerns the genital zones proper; these in turn transmit their excitation to the other erogenous zones, usually dormant in mature life, which the behave exactly like genitals.

But besides this, just as in thumbsucking, any other region of the body may become endowed with the excitation of the genitals and raised to an erogenous zone. Erogenous and hysterogenous zones show the same characters.[10]

The Infantile Sexual Aim.—The sexual aim of the infantile impulse consists in the production of gratification through the proper excitation of this or that selected erogenous zone. In order to leave a desire for its repetition this gratification must have been previously experienced, and we may be sure that nature has devised definite means so as not to leave this occurrence to mere chance. The arrangement which has fulfilled this purpose for the lip-zone we have already discussed; it is the simultaneous connection of this part of the body with the taking of nourishment. We shall also meet other similar mechanisms as sources of sexuality. The state of desire for repetition of gratification can be recognized through a peculiar feeling of tension which in itself is rather of a painful character, and through a centrally-determined feeling of itching or sensitiveness which is projected into the peripheral erogenous zone. The sexual aim may therefore be formulated as follows: the chief object is to substitute for the projected feeling of sensitiveness in the erogenous zone that outer stimulus which removes the feeling of sensitiveness by evoking the feeling of gratification. This external stimulus consists usually in a manifestation which is analogous to sucking.

It is in full accord with our physiological knowledge if the desire happens to be awakened also peripherally through an actual change in the erogenous zone. The action is only to some extent strange, as one stimulus for its suppression seems to want another applied to the same place.

---

[9] The biological problems connected with the formation of the ero-genous zones are discussed by Alfred Adler in his Studien uber Minder-wertigkeit von Organen, Wien, 1907.

The Masturbatic Sexual Manifestations[11]

It is a matter of great satisfaction to know that there is nothing further of greater importance to learn about the sexual activity of the child after the impulse of one erogenous zone has become comprehensible to us. The most pronounced differences are found in the action necessary for the gratification, which consists in sucking for the lip-zone and which must be replaced by other muscular actions according to the situation and nature of the other zones.

The Activity of the Anal Zone.—Like the lip zone the anal zone is, through its position, adapted to conduct the sexuality to the other functions of the body. It should be assumed that the erogenous significance of this region of the body was originally very large. Through psychoanalysis one finds, not without surprise, the many transformations that are normally undertaken with the usual excitations emanating from here, and that this zone often retains for life a considerable fragment of genital irritability.[12] The intestinal catarrhs so frequent during infancy produce intensive irritations in this zone, and we often hear it said that intestinal catarrh at this delicate age causes "nervousness." In later neurotic diseases they exert a definite influence on the symptomatic expression of the neurosis, placing at its disposal the whole sum of intestinal disturbances. Considering the erogenous significance of the anal zone which has been retained at least in transformation, one should not laugh at the hemorrhoidal influences to which the old medical literature attached so much weight in the explanation of neurotic states.

Children utilizing the erogenous sensitiveness of the anal zone can be recognized by their holding back of fecal masses until through accumulation there result violent muscular contractions;

[11] Compare here the very comprehensive but confusing literature on onanism, e. g., Rohleder, Die Masturbation, 1899.

[12] Compare here the essay on "Charakter und Analerotic" in the Sammlung kleiner Schriften zur Neurosenlehre, Zweite Folge, 1909.

the passage of these masses through the anus is apt to produce a marked irritation on the mucus membrane. Besides the pain this must produce also a sensation of pleasure. One of the surest premonitions of later eccentricity or nervousness is when an infant obstinately refuses to empty his bowel when placed on the chamber by the nurse and reserves this function at its own pleasure. It does not concern him that he will soil his bed; all he cares for is not to lose the subsidiary pleasure while defecating. The educators have again the right inkling when they designate children who withhold these functions as bad.

The retention of fecal masses, which is at first intentional in order to utilize them, as it were, for masturbatic excitation of the anal zone, is at least one of the roots of constipation so frequent in neuropaths. The whole significance of the anal zone is mirrored in the fact that there are but few neurotics who have not their special scatologic customs, ceremonies, etc., which they retain with cautious secrecy.

Real masturbatic irritation of the anal zone by means of the fingers, evoked through either centrally or peripherally supported itching, is not at all rare in older children.

The Activity of the Genital Zone.—Among the erogenous zones of the child's body there is one which certainly does not play the main rôle, and which cannot be the carrier of earliest sexual feeling—which, however, is destined for great things in the later life. In both male and female it is connected with the voiding of urine (penis, clitoris), and in the former it is enclosed in a sack of mucous membrane, probably in order not to miss the irritations caused by the secretions which may arouse the sexual excitement at an early age. The sexual activities of this erogenous zone, which belongs to the real genitals, are the beginning of the later normal sexual life.

Owing to the anatomical position, the overflowing of secretions, the washing and rubbing of the body, and to certain accidental excitements (the wandering of intestinal worms in the girl), it happens that the pleasurable feeling which these parts of the body are capable of producing makes itself noticeable to the child even during the sucking age, and thus awakens desire for its repetition. When we review all the actual arrangements, and bear in mind that the measures for cleanliness have the same effect as the uncleanliness itself, we can then scarcely mistake nature's intention, which is to establish the future primacy of these erogenous zones for the sexual activity through the infantile onanism from which hardly an individual escapes.¹ The action removing the stimulus and setting free the gratification consists in a rubbing contiguity with the hand or in a certain previously-formed pressure reflex effected by the closure of the thighs. The latter procedure seems to be the more primitive and is by far the more common in girls. The preference for the hand in boys already indicates what an important part of the male sexual activity will be accomplished in the future by the acquisition impulse (Bemächtigungstrieb). ⟶

The infantile onanism seems to disappear with the onset of the latency period, but it may continue uninterruptedly till puberty and thus represent the first marked deviation from the development desirable for civilized man. At some time during childhood after the nursing period, the sexual impulse of the genitals reawakens and continues active for some time until it is again suppressed, or it may continue without interruption. The possible relations are very diverse and can only be elucidated through a more precise analysis of individual cases. The details, however, of this second infantile sexual activity leave behind the profoundest (unconscious) impressions in the person's memory; if the individual remains healthy they determine his character and if he becomes sick after puberty they determine the symptomatology of his neurosis. In the latter case it is found that this sexual period is forgotten and the conscious reminiscences pointing to them are displaced; I have already mentioned that I would like to connect the normal infantile amnesia with this infantile sexual activity. By psychoanalytic investigation it is possible to bring to consciousness the forgotten material, and thereby to remove a compulsion which emanates from the unconscious psychic material.

The Return of the Infantile Masturbation.—The sexual excitation of the infantile period returns during childhood (we have not yet succeeded in establishing definite periods), either as a centrally determined tickling sensation demanding onanistic gratification, or as a pollution-like process which, analogous to the pollution of maturity, may attain gratification without the aid of any action. The latter case is more frequent in girls and in the second half of childhood; its determinants are not well understood, but it often, though not regularly seems to have as a basis a period of early active onanism. The symptomatology of this sexual manifestation is poor; the genital apparatus is still undeveloped and all signs are therefore displayed by the urinary apparatus which is, so to say, the guardian of the genital apparatus. Most of the so-called bladder disturbances of this period are of a sexual nature; whenever the enuresis nocturna does not represent an epileptic attack it corresponds to a pollution.

The return of the sexual activity is determined by inner and outer causes which can be conjectured from the formation of the symptoms of neurotic diseases and definitely revealed by psychoanalytic investigations. The internal causes will be discussed later; the accidental outer causes attain at this time a great and permanent significance. As the first outer cause we have the influence of seduction which prematurely treats the child as a sexual object; under conditions favoring impressions this teaches the child the gratification of the genital zones, and thus usually forces it to repeat this gratification in onanism. Such influences can come from adults or other children. I cannot admit that I over-estimated its frequency or its significance in my contribu_ tions to the etiology of hysteria,[13] though I did not know then that normal individuals may have the same experiences in their childhood, and hence placed a higher value on seductions than on the factors found in the sexual constitution and development.[14] It is quite obvious that no seduction is necessary to awaken the sexual life of the child, that such an awakening may come on spontaneously from inner sources.

Polymorphous-perverse Disposition.—It is instructive to know that under the influence of seduction the child may become polymorphous-perverse and may be misled into all sorts of trans- gressions. This goes to show that it carries along the adaptation for them in its disposition. The formation of such perversions meets but slight resistance because the psychic dams against sexual excesses, such as shame, loathing and morality—which depend on the age of the child—are not yet erected or are only in the process of formation. In this respect the child perhaps does not behave differently from the average uncivilized woman in whom the same polymorphous-perverse disposition exists. Such a woman may remain sexually normal under usual conditions, but under the guidance of a clever seducer she will find pleasure in every perversion, and will retain the same as her sexual activity. The same polymorphous or infantile disposition fits the prostitute for her professional activity, and in the enormous number of prosti-

[13] Freud, Selected Papers on Hysteria & Other Psychoneuroses, translated by A. A. Brill, Ph.B., M.D.; N. Y. Jour. Nerv. & Ment. Dis. Pub. Co. Nervous and Mental Disease Monograph, Series No. 4.

[14] Havelock Ellis in an appendix to his study on the Sexual Impulse, 1903, gives a number of autobiographic reports of normal persons treating their first sexual feelings in childhood and the causes of the same. These reports naturally show the deficiency due to infantile amnesia; they do not cover the prehistoric time in the sexual life and therefore must be supplemented by psychoanalysis of individuals who became neurotic. Notwithstanding this these reports are valuable in more than one respect, and information of a similar nature has urged me to modify my etiological assumption. as mentioned in the text.

4

tutes and of women to whom we must attribute an adaptation for prostitution, even if they do not follow this calling, it is absolutely impossible not to recognize in their uniform disposition for all perversions the universal and primitive human.

Partial Impulses.—For the rest, the influence of seduction does not aid us in unravelling the original relations of the sexual impulse, but rather confuses our understanding of the same, inasmuch as it prematurely supplies the child with the sexual object at a time when the infantile sexual impulse does not yet evince any desire for it. We must admit, however, that the infantile sexual life, though mainly under the control of erogenous zones, also shows components in which from the very beginning other persons are regarded as sexual objects. Among these we have the impulses for looking and showing, and for cruelty, which manifest themselves somewhat independently of the erogenous zones and which only later enter into intimate relationship with the sexual life; but along with the erogenous sexual activity they are noticeable even in the infantile years as separate and independent strivings. The little child is above all shameless, and during its early years it sometimes evinces pleasure in displaying its body and especially its sexual organs. A counterpart to this desire which is to be considered as perverse, the curiosity to see other persons' genitals, probably appears first in the later years of childhood when the hindrance of the feeling of shame has already reached a certain development. Under the influence of seduction the looking perversion may attain great importance for the sexual life of the child. Still, from my investigations of the childhood years of normal and neurotic patients, I must conclude that the impulse for looking can appear in the child as a spontaneous sexual manifestation. Small children, whose attention has once been directed to their own genitals—usually by masturbation—are wont to progress in this direction without outside interference, and to develop a vivid interest in the genitals of their playmates. As the occasion for the gratification of such curiosity is generally afforded during the gratification of both excrementitious needs, such children become voyeurs and are zealous spectators at the voiding of urine and feces of others. After this tendency has been repressed, the curiosity to see the genitals of others (one's own or those of the other sex), remains as a tormenting desire which in some neurotic cases furnishes the strongest motive power for the formation of symptoms.

The cruelty component of the sexual impulse develops in the child with still greater independence of those sexual activities which are connected with erogenous zones. Cruelty is especially near the childish character, since the inhibition which restrains the acquisition impulse through the influence of others—that is, the capacity for sympathy—develops comparatively late. As we know, a thorough psychological analysis of this impulse has not as yet been successfully accomplished; we may assume that the cruel feelings emanate from sources which are actually independent of sexuality but with which an early connection is formed through an anastomosis near the origins of both. But observation shows that relations exist between the sexual development and the looking and cruelty impulses which restrict the pretended independence of both impulses. Children who are distinguished for evincing especial cruelty to animals and playmates may be justly suspected of intensive and premature sexual activity in the erogenous zones; and in a simultaneous prematurity of all sexual impulses, the erogenous sexual activity surely seems to be primary. The absence of the barrier of sympathy carries with it the danger that the connections between cruelty and the erogenous impulses formed in childhood cannot be broken in later life.

An erogenous source of the passive impulse for cruelty (masochism) is found in the painful irritation of the gluteal region which is familiar to all educators since the confessions of J. J. Rousseau. This has justly caused them to demand that physical punishment, which usually concerns this part of the body, should be withheld from all children in whom the libido might be forced into collateral roads by the later demands of cultural education.[15]

THE SOURCES OF THE INFANTILE SEXUALITY

In our effort to follow up the origins of the sexual impulse, we have thus far found that the sexual excitement originates (*a*) in an imitation of a gratification which has been experienced in conjunction with other organic processes; (*b*) through the appro-

---

[15] The above-mentioned assertions concerning the infantile sexuality were justified in 1905, in the main through the results of psychoanalytic investigations in adults. Direct observation of the child could not at the time be utilized to its full extent and resulted only in individual indications and valuable confirmations. Since then it has become possible through the analysis of some cases of nervous disease in the delicate age of childhood to gain a direct understanding of the infantile psychosexuality (Jahrbuch für psychoanalytische und psychopathische Forschungen, Bd. I, 2, 1909). I can point with satisfaction to the fact that direct observation has fully confirmed the conclusion drawn from psychoanalysis, and thus furnishes good evidence for the reliability of the latter method of investigation.

Moreover the "Analysis of a Phobia in a Five-year-old Boy" (Jahrbuch, Bd. I) has taught us something new for which psychoanalysis had not prepared us to wit, that sexual symbolism, the representation of the sexual by non-sexual objects and relations—reaches back into the years when the child is first learning to master the language. My attention has also been directed to a deficiency in the above-cited statement which for the sake of clearness described any conceivable separation between the two phases of autoerotism and object love as a temporal separation. From the cited analysis (as well as from the above-mentioned work of Bell) we learn that children from three to five are capable of evincing a very strong object-selection which is accompanied by strong affects.

Another amplification of our knowledge of the sexual life of children not hitherto mentioned in the text is found in the infantile sexual investigations (compare the paper "Concerning Infantile Sexual Theories," in the Sammlung kleiner Schriften zur Neurosenlehre, zweite Folge). This paper treats of the theories held by the children themselves, the importance of these theories for later neuroses, the fate of these childish investigations, and their relations to the development of the infantile mind.

priate peripheral stimulation of erogenous zones; (c) and as an expression of some "impulse," like the looking and cruelty impulses, the origin of which we do not yet fully understand. The psychoanalytic investigation of later life which leads back to childhood and the contemporary observation of the child itself coöperate to reveal to us still other regularly-flowing sources of the sexual excitement. The observation of childhood has the disadvantage of treating easily misunderstood material, while psychoanalysis is made difficult by the fact that it can reach its objects and conclusions only by great detours; still the united efforts of both methods achieve a sufficient degree of positive understanding.

In investigating the erogenous zones we have already found that these skin regions merely show the special exaggeration of a form of sensitiveness which is to a certain degree found over the whole surface of the skin. It will therefore not surprise us to learn that certain forms of general sensitiveness in the skin can be ascribed to very distinct erogenous action. Among these we will above all mention the temperature sensitiveness; this will perhaps prepare us for the understanding of the therapeutic effects of warm baths.

Mechanical Excitation.—We must, moreover, describe here the production of sexual excitation by means of rhythmic mechanical shaking of the body. There are three kinds of exciting influences: those acting on the sensory apparatus of the vestibular nerves, those acting on the skin, and those acting on the deep parts, such as the muscles and joints. The sexual excitation produced by these influences seems to be of a pleasurable nature— a problem to which we will direct our attention later—and that the pleasure is produced by mechanical stimulation is proved by the fact that children are so fond of play involving passive motion, like swinging or flying in the air, and repeatedly demand its repetition.[10] As we know, rocking is regularly used in putting

[10] Some persons can recall that the contact of the moving air in swinging caused them direct sexual pleasure in the genitals.

to sleep restless children. The shaking sensation experienced in wagons and railroad trains exerts such a fascinating influence on older children, that all boys, at least at one time in their lives, want to become conductors and drivers. They are wont to ascribe to railroad activities an extraordinary and mysterious interest, and during the age of phantastic activity (shortly before puberty) they utilize these as a nucleus for exquisite sexual symbolisms. The desire to connect railroad travelling with sexuality apparently originates from the pleasurable character of the sensation of motion. .When the repression later sets in and changes so many of the childish likes into their opposites, these same persons as adolescents and adults then react to the rocking and rolling with nausea and become terribly exhausted by a railroad journey, or they show a tendency to attacks of anxiety during the journey, and by becoming obsessed with railroad phobia they protect themselves against a repetition of the painful experiences.

This also fits in with the not as yet understood fact that the concurrence of fear with mechanical shaking produces the severest hysterical forms of traumatic neurosis. It may at least be assumed that inasmuch as even a slight intensity of these influences becomes a source of sexual excitement, the action of an excessive amount of the same will produce a profound disorder in the sexual mechanism.

Muscular Activity.—It is well known that the child has need for strong muscular activity, from the gratification of which it draws extraordinary pleasure. Whether this pleasure has anything to do with sexuality, whether it includes in itself sexual gratification, or can become a cause of sexual excitement, all these problems may be solved by critical reflection, which will no doubt also be directed toward the statements made above, namely, that the sensations of passive motion are of a sexual nature or produce sexual excitement. The fact remains, however, that a number of persons report that they experienced the first signs of excitement in their genitals during fighting or wrestling with playmates, in which situation, besides the general muscular exertion, there is an intensive contact with the opponent's skin which also becomes effective. The desire for muscular contest with a definite person, like the desire for word contest in later years, is a good sign that the object selection has been directed upon this person. "Was sich liebt, das neckt sich."[17] In the promotion of sexual excitement through muscular activity we might recognize one of the sources of the sadistic impulse. The infantile connection between fighting and sexual excitement acts in many persons as a future determinant for the preferred course of their sexual impulse.[18]

Affective Processes.—The other sources of sexual excitement in the child are open to less doubt. Through simultaneous observations, as well as through later investigations, it is easy to ascertain that all more intensive affective processes, even excitements of a terrifying nature, encroach upon sexuality; this can at all events furnish us with a contribution to the understanding of the pathogenic action of such emotions. In the school child, fear of a coming examination or exertion expended in the solution of a difficult task can become significant for the breaking through of sexual manifestations as well as for his relations to the school, inasmuch as under such excitements a sensation often occurs urging him to touch the genitals, or leading to a pollution-like process with all its disagreeable consequences. The behavior of children at school, which is so often mysterious to the teacher, ought surely to be considered in relation with their germinating sexuality. The sexually-exciting influence of some painful affects,

---

[17] "Those who love each other tease each other."

[18] The analyses of neurotic disturbances of walking and of agoraphobia remove all doubt as to the sexual nature of the pleasure of motion. As everybody knows modern cultural education utilizes sports to a great extent in order to turn away the youth from sexual activity; it would be more proper to say that it replaces the sexual pleasure by motion pleasure, and forces the sexual activity back upon one of its autoerotic components.

such as fear, shuddering, and horror, is felt by a great many people throughout life and readily explains why so many seek opportunities to experience such sensations, provided that certain accessory circumstances (as in fiction, reading, the theater) suppress the earnestness of the painful feeling.

If we might assume that the same erogenous action also reaches the intensive painful feelings, especially if the pain be toned down or held at a distance by a subsidiary determination, this relation would then contain the main roots of the masochistic-sadistic impulse, into the manifold composition of which we are gaining a gradual insight.

Intellectual Work.—Finally, it is evident that mental application or the concentration of attention on an intellectual accomplishment will result, especially often in youthful persons, but in older persons as well, in a simultaneous sexual excitement, which may be looked upon as the only justified basis for the otherwise so doubtful etiology of nervous disturbances from mental " overwork."

If we now, in conclusion, review the evidences and indications of the sources of the infantile sexual excitement, which have been reported neither completely nor exhaustively, we may lay down the following general laws as suggested or established. It seems to be provided in the most generous manner that the process of sexual excitement—the nature of which certainly remains quite mysterious to us—should be set in motion. The factor making this provision in a more or less direct way is the excitation of the sensible surfaces of the skin and sensory organs, while the most indirect exciting influences are exerted on certain parts which are designated as erogenous zones. The criterion in all these sources of sexual excitement is really the quality of the stimuli, though the factor of intensity (in pain) is not entirely unimportant. But in addition to this there are arrangements in the organism which cause the origin of the sexual excitement as a subsidiary action in a large number of inner processes as soon as the intensity of these processes has risen above certain quantitative limits. What we have designated as the partial impulses of sexuality are either directly derived from these inner sources of sexual excitation or composed of contributions from such sources and from erogenous zones. It is possible that nothing of any considerable significance occurs in the organism that does not contribute its components to the excitement of the sexual impulse.

It seems to me at present impossible to shed more light and certainty on these general propositions, and for this I hold two factors responsible; first, the novelty of this manner of investigation, and secondly, the fact that the nature of the sexual excitement is entirely unfamiliar to us. Nevertheless, I will not forbear speaking about two points which promise to open wide prospects in the future.

Diverse Sexual Constitutions.—(a) We have considered above the possibility of establishing the manifold character of congenital sexual constitutions through the diverse formation of the erogenous zones; we may now attempt to do the same in dealing with the indirect sources of sexual excitement. We may assume that, although these different sources furnish contributions in all individuals, they are not all equally strong in all persons; and that a further contribution to the differentiation of the diverse sexual constitution will be found in the preferred developments of the individual sources of sexual excitement. ·

The Roads of Opposite Influences.—(b) Since we are now dropping the figurative manner of expression hitherto employed, by which we spoke of *sources* of sexual excitement, we may now assume that all the connecting ways leading from other functions to sexuality must also be passable in the reverse direction. For example, if the lip zone, the common possession of both functions, is responsible for the fact that the sexual gratification originates during the taking of nourishment, the same factor offers also an explanation for the disturbances in the taking of nourishment if the erogenous functions of the common zone are disturbed.   As soon as we know that concentration of attention may produce sexual excitement, it is quite natural to assume that acting on the same road, but in a contrary direction, the state of sexual excitement will be able to influence the availability of the voluntary attention.   A good part of the symptomatology of the neuroses which I trace to disturbance of sexual processes manifests itself in other non-sexual bodily functions, and this hitherto incomprehensible action becomes less mysterious if it only represents the counterpart of the influences controlling the production of the sexual excitement.

However the same roads through which sexual disturbances encroach upon the other functions of the body must in health be supposed to serve another important function.   It must be through these roads that the attraction of the sexual motive powers to other than sexual aims, the sublimation of sexuality, is accomplished.   We must conclude with the admission that very little is definitely known concerning the roads beyond the fact that they exist, and that they are probably passable in both directions.

III

THE TRANSFORMATION OF PUBERTY

With the beginning of puberty the changes set in which transform the infantile sexual life into its definite normal form. Hitherto the sexual impulse has been preponderately autoerotic; it now finds the sexual object. Thus far it has manifested itself in single impulses and in erogenous zones seeking a certain pleasure as a single sexual aim. A new sexual aim now appears for the production of which all partial impulses coöperate, while the erogenous zones subordinate themselves under the primacy of the genital zone. As the new sexual aim assigns very different functions to the two sexes their sexual developments now part company. The sexual development of the man is more consistent and easier to understand, while in the woman there even appears a form of regression. The normality of the sexual life is guaranteed only by the exact concurrence of the two streams directed to the sexual object and sexual aim. It is like the piercing of a tunnel from opposite sides.

The new sexual aim in the man consists in the discharging of the sexual products; it is not markedly different from the former sexual aim in its manner of obtaining pleasure; on the contrary, the highest amount of pleasure is connected with this final act in the sexual process. The sexual impulse now enters into the service of the function of propagation; it becomes, so to say, altruistic. If this transformation is to succeed its process must be adjusted to the original dispositions and all the peculiarities of the impulses.

Just as on every other occasion where new connections and compositions are to be formed in complicated mechanisms, here,

too, there is a possibility of morbid disturbance if the new order
of things does not take place.

THE PRIMACY OF THE GENITAL ZONES AND THE FORE-PLEASURE

From the course of development as described we can clearly
see the issue and the end aim. The intermediary transitions are
still quite obscure and many a riddle will have to be solved in
them.

The most striking process of puberty has been selected as its
most characteristic; it is the manifest growth of the external
genitals which have shown a relative inhibition of growth during
the latency period of childhood. Simultaneously the inner genitals develop to such an extent as to be able to furnish sexual
products for the reception and formation of a new living being.
A most complicated apparatus is thus formed which waits to be
claimed.

This apparatus can be set in motion by stimuli, and observation teaches that the stimuli can affect it in three ways: from the
outer world through the familiar erogenous zones; from the inner
organic world by ways still to be investigated; and from the
psychic life, which merely represents a depository of external
impressions and a receptacle of inner excitations. The same
result follows in all three cases, namely, a state which can be
designated as " sexual excitation " and which manifests itself in
psychic and somatic signs. The psychic sign consists in a peeu-
liar feeling of tension of a most urgent character, and among
the manifold somatic signs the many changes in the genitals stand
first. They have a definite meaning, that of readiness; they con-
stitute a preparation for the sexual act (the erection of the penis,
and the glandular activity of the vagina).

The Sexual Tension.—The character of the tension of sexual
excitation is connected with a problem the solution of which
would be difficult but important for the conception of the sexual
process. Despite all divergence of opinion regarding it in psy.

chology, I must firmly maintain that a feeling of tension must carry with it the character of displeasure. For me it is conclusive that such a feeling carries with it the impulse to alter the psychic situation, and acts incitingly, which is quite contrary to the nature of perceived pleasure. But if we ascribe the tension of the sexual excitation to the feelings of displeasure we encounter the fact that it is undoubtedly pleasurably perceived. The tension produced by sexual excitation is everywhere accompanied by pleasure; even in the preparatory changes of the genitals there is a distinct feeling of satisfaction. What relation is there between this unpleasant tension and this feeling of pleasure?

Everything relating to the problem of pleasure and pain touches one of the weakest spots of present-day psychology. We shall try if possible to learn something from the determinations of the case in question and to avoid encroaching on the problem as a whole. Let us first glance at the manner in which the erogenous zones adjust themselves to the new order of things. An important rôle devolves upon them in the preparation of the sexual excitation. The eye which is very remote from the sexual object, is most often in position, during the relations of object wooing, to become attracted by that particular quality of excitation, the motive of which we designate as beauty in the sexual object. The excellencies of the sexual object are therefore also called "attractions." This excitation is on the one hand already connected with pleasure, ánd on the other hand it either results in an increase of the sexual excitation or in an evocation of the same where it is still wanting. The effect is the same if the excitation of another erogenous zone, e. g., the touching hand, is added to it. There is on the one hand the feeling of pleasure which soon becomes enhanced by the pleasure from the preparatory changes, and on the other hand there is a further increase of the sexual tension which soon changes into a most distinct feeling of displeasure if it cannot proceed to more pleasure. Another case will perhaps be clearer; let us, for example, take the case where an erogenous zone, like a woman's breast, is excited by touching in a person who is not sexually excited at the time. This touching in itself evokes a feeling of pleasure, but nothing is better adapted to awaken sexual excitement which demands a greater portion of pleasure. How it happens that the perceived pleasure evokes the desire for greater pleasure, that is the real problem.

Fore-pleasure Mechanism.—But the rôle which devolves upon the erogenous zones is clear. What applies to one applies to all. They are all utilized to furnish a certain amount of pleasure through their own proper excitation, which increases the tension, and which is in turn destined to produce the necessary motor energy in order to bring to a conclusion the sexual act. The last part but one of this act is again a suitable excitation of an erogenous zone; *i. e.,* the genital zone proper of the glans penis is excited by the object most fit for it, the mucous membrane of the vagina, and through the pleasure furnished by this excitation it now produces reflexly the motor energy which conveys to the surface the sexual substance. This last pleasure is highest in its intensity, and differs from the earliest ones in its mechanism. It is altogether produced through discharge and it is altogether a pleasure of gratification; the tension of the libido temporarily dies away with it.

It does not seem to me unauthorized to fix by name the distinction in the nature of these pleasures, the one through the excitation of the erogenous zones, and the other through the discharge of the sexual substance. In contradistinction to the end-pleasure, or pleasure of gratification of sexual activity, we can properly designate the first as fore-pleasure. The fore-pleasure is then the same as that furnished by the infantile sexual impulse, though on a reduced scale; while the end-pleasure is new and is probably connected with determinations which first appear in puberty. The formula for the new function of the erogenous zones reads as follows: they are utilized for the purpose of

making possible the production of the greater pleasure of gratification by means of the fore-pleasure which is gained from them
as in infantile life.

I have recently been able to elucidate another example from a
quite different realm of the psychic life, in which likewise a
greater feeling of pleasure is achieved by means of a lesser feeling of pleasure which acts as an alluring premium. We had
there also the opportunity of entering more deeply into the nature
of pleasure.[1]

Dangers of the Fore-pleasure.—However the connection of
fore-pleasure with the infantile life is strengthened by the pathogenic rôle which may devolve upon it. The mechanism shelter-
ing the fore-pleasure may result in a danger for the attainment of
the normal sexual aim. This occurs if it happens that there is
too much fore-pleasure and too little tension on any part of the
preparatory sexual process. The motive power for the further
continuation of the sexual process then escapes, the whole road
becomes shortened, and the preparatory action in question takes
the place of the normal sexual aim. Experience shows that such
a hurtful case is determined by the fact that the erogenous zone
concerned or the corresponding partial impulse has already con-
tributed an unusual amount of pleasure in infantile life. If other
factors favoring fixation are added a compulsion readily results
for the later life which prevents the fore-pleasure from arrang-
ing itself into a new combination. Indeed, the mechanism of
many perversions is of such a nature; they merely represent a
lingering at a preparatory act of the sexual process.

The failure of the function of the sexual mechanism through
the fault of the fore-pleasure is generally avoided if the primacy
of the genital zones has also already been sketched out in infantile life. The preparations of the second half of childhood (from

[1] See my work "Der Witz und seine Beziehung zum Unbewussten":
"The fore-pleasure gained by the technique of wit is utilized for the purpose of setting free a greater pleasure by the removal of inner inhibitions."

the eighth year to puberty) really seem to favor this. During these years the genital zones behave almost as at the age of maturity; they are the seat of exciting sensations and of preparatory changes if any kind of pleasure is experienced through the gratification of other erogenous zones; although this effect remains aimless, *i. e.,* it contributes nothing towards the continuation of the sexual process. Besides the pleasure of gratification a certain amount of sexual tension appears even in infancy, though it is less constant and less abundant. We can now understand also why in the discussion of the sources of sexuality we had a perfectly good reason for saying that the process in question acts as sexual gratification as well as sexual excitement. We note that on our way towards the truth we have at first enormously exaggerated the distinctions between the infantile and the mature sexual life, and we therefore supplement what has been said with a correction. The infantile manifestations of sexuality determine not only the deviations from the normal sexual life but also the normal formations of the same.

The Problem of Sexual Excitement

It remained to us above entirely unexplained whence the sexual tension comes which originates simultaneously with the gratification of erogenous zones and what is its nature. The obvious supposition that this tension originates in some way from the pleasure itself is not only improbable in itself but untenable, inasmuch as during the greatest pleasure which is connected with the voiding of sexual substance there is no production of tension but rather a removal of all tension. Hence, pleasure and sexual tension can be only indirectly connected.

The Rôle of the Sexual Substance.—Aside from the fact that only the discharge of the sexual substance can normally put an end to the sexual excitement, there are other essential facts which bring the sexual tension into relation with the sexual products. In a life of continence the sexual activity is wont to discharge the sexual substance at night during pleasurable dream hallucinations of a sexual act, this discharge coming at changing but not at entirely capricious intervals; and the following interpretation of this process—the nocturnal pollution—can hardly be rejected, viz., that the sexual tension which brings about a substitute for the sexual act by the short hallucinatory road is a function of the accumulated semen in the reservoirs for the sexual products. Experiences with the exhaustibility of the sexual mechanism speak for the same thing. Where there is no stock of semen it is not only impossible to accomplish the sexual act, but there is also a lack of excitability in the erogenous zones, the suitable excitation of which can evoke no pleasure. We thus discover incidentally that a certain amount of sexual tension is itself necessary for the excitability of the erogenous zones.

One is thus forced to the assumption, which if I am not mistaken is quite generally adopted, that the accumulation of sexual substance produces and maintains the sexual tension. The pressure of these products on the walls of their receptacles acts as an excitant on the spinal center, the state of which is then perceived by the higher centers which then produce in consciousness the familiar feeling of tension. If the excitation of erogenous zones increases the sexual tension, it can only be due to the fact that the erogenous zones are connected with these centers by previously formed anatomical connections. They increase there the tone of the excitation, and with sufficient sexual tension they set in motion the sexual act, and with insufficient tension they merely stimulate a production of the sexual substance.

The weakness of the theory which one finds adopted, e. g., in v. Krafft-Ebing's description of the sexual process, lies in the fact that it has been formed for the sexual activity of the mature man and pays too little heed to three kinds of relations which should also have been elucidated. We refer to the relations as found in the child, in the woman, and in the castrated male. In none of the three cases can we speak of an accumulation of sexual products in the same sense as in the man, which naturally renders difficult the general application of this scheme; still it may be admitted without any further ado that ways can be found to justify the subordination of even these cases. At all events one should be cautious about burdening the factor of accumulation of sexual products with actions which it seems incapable of supporting.

Overestimation of the Internal Genitals.—That sexual excitement can be to a considerable extent independent of the production of sexual substance seems to be shown by observations on castrated males, in whom the libido sometimes escapes the injury caused by the operation, although the opposite behavior, which is really the motive for the operation, is usually the rule. It is therefore not at all surprising, as C. Rieger puts it, that the loss of the male germ glands in maturer age should exert no new influence on the psychic life of the individual. The germ glands are really not the sexuality, and the experience with castrated males only verifies what we had long before learned from the removal of the ovaries, namely, that it is impossible to do away with the sexual character by removing the germ glands. To be sure, castration performed at a delicate age, before puberty, comes nearer to this aim, but it would seem in this case that besides the loss of the sexual glands we must also consider the inhibition of development and other factors which are connected with that loss.

Chemical Theories.—The truth remains, however, that we are unable to give any information about the nature of the sexual excitement for the reason that we do not know with what organ or organs sexuality is connected, since we have seen that the sexual glands have been overestimated in this significance. Since surprising discoveries have taught us the important rôle of the thyroid gland in sexuality, we may assume that the knowledge of the essential factors of sexuality are still withheld from us. One who feels the need of filling up the large gap in our knowledge with a preliminary assumption may formulate for himself the following theory based on the active substances found in the thyroid. Through the adapted excitement of erogenous zones, as well as through other conditions under which sexual excitement originates, a material which is universally distributed in the organism becomes disintegrated, the decomposing products of which supply a specific stimulus to the organs of reproduction or to the spinal center connected with them. Such a transformation of a toxic stimulus in a particular organic stimulus we are already familiar with from other toxic products introduced into the body from without. To treat, if only hypothetically, the complexities of the pure toxic and the physiologic stimulations which result in the sexual processes is not now our appropriate task. To be sure, I attach no value to this special assumption and I shall be quite ready to give it up in favor of another, provided its original character, the emphasis on the sexual chemism, were preserved. For this apparently arbitrary statement is supported by a fact which, though little heeded, is most noteworthy. The neuroses which can be traced only to disturbances of the sexual life show the greatest clinical resemblance to the phenomena of intoxication and abstinence which result through the habitual introduction of pleasure-producing poisonous substances (alkaloids).

DIFFERENTIATION BETWEEN MAN AND WOMAN

It is known that the sharp differentiation of the male and female character originates at puberty, and it is the resulting difference which, more than any other factor, decisively influences the later development of personality. To be sure, the male and female dispositions are easily recognizable even in infantile life; thus the development of sexual inhibitions (shame, loathing, sympathy, etc.) ensues earlier and with less resistance in the little girl than in the little boy. The tendency to sexual repression certainly seems much greater, and where partial impulses of sexuality are noticed they show a preference for the passive form. But the autoerotic activity of the erogenous zones is the same in both sexes, and it is this agreement that removes the possibility of a sex differentiation in childhood as it appears after puberty. In respect to the autoerotic and masturbatic sexual manifestations, it may be asserted that the sexuality of the little girl has entirely a male character. Indeed, if one could give a more definite content to the terms " masculine and feminine," one might advance the opinion that *the libido is regularly and lawfully of a masculine nature, be it in the man or in the woman; and if we consider its object, this may be either the man or the woman.*

Since becoming acquainted with the aspect of bisexuality I hold this factor as here decisive, and I believe that without taking into account the factor of bisexuality it will hardly be possible to understand the actually observed sexual manifestations in man and woman.

The Leading Zones in Man and Woman.—Further than this I can only add the following. The chief erogenous zone in the female child is the clitoris, which is homologous to the male penis. All I have been able to discover concerning masturbation in little girls concerned the clitoris and not those other external genitals which are so important for the later sexual functions. With few exceptions I myself doubt whether the female child can be seduced to anything but clitoris masturbation. The frequent spontaneous discharges of sexual excitement in little girls manifest themselves in a twitching of the clitoris, and the frequent erections of the same enable the girl to understand correctly even without any instruction the sexual manifestations of the other sex; they simply transfer to the boys the sensations of their own sexual processes.

If one wishes to understand how the little girl becomes a woman, he must follow up the further destinies of this clitoris excitation. Puberty, which brings to the boy a great advance of libido, distinguishes itself in the girl by a new wave of repression which especially concerns the clitoris sexuality. It is a part of the male sexual life that merges into repression. The reënforcement of the sexual inhibitions produced in the woman by the repression of puberty causes a stimulus in the libido of the man and forces it to increase its capacity; with the height of the libido there is a rise in the overestimation of the sexual, which can be present in its full force only when the woman refuses and denies her sexuality. If the sexual act is finally submitted to and the clitoris becomes excited its rôle is then to conduct the excitement to the adjacent female parts, and in this it acts like a chip of pine wood which is utilized to set fire to the harder wood. It often takes some time for this transference to be accomplished, during which the young wife remains anesthetic. This anesthesia may become permanent if the clitoris zone refuses to give up its excitability; a condition brought on by abundant activities in infantile life. It is known that anesthesia in women is often only apparent and local. They are anesthetic at the vaginal entrance but not at all unexcitable through the clitoris or even through other zones. Besides these erogenous causes of anesthesia there are also psychic causes likewise determined by the repression.

If the transference of the erogenous excitability from the clitoris to the vagina has succeeded, the woman has thus changed her leading zone for the future sexual activity; the man on the other hand retains his from childhood. The main determinants for the woman's preference for the neuroses, especially for hysteria, lie in this change of the leading zone as well as in the repression of puberty. These determinants are therefore most intimately connected with the nature of femininity.

THE OBJECT-FINDING

While the primacy of the genital zones is being established through the processes of puberty, and the erected penis in the man imperiously points towards the new sexual aim, i. e., towards the penetration of a cavity which excites the genital zone, the object-finding, for which also preparations have been made since early childhood, becomes consummated on the psychic side. While the very incipient sexual gratifications are still connected with the taking of nourishment, the sexual impulse has a sexual object outside its own body in his mother's breast. This object it loses later, perhaps at the very time when it becomes possible for the child to form a general picture of the person to whom the organ granting him the gratification belongs. The sexual impulse later regularly becomes autoerotic, and only after overcoming the latency period is there a resumption of the original relation. It is not without good reason that the suckling of the child from its mother's breast has become a model for every amour. The object-finding is really a re-finding.

The **Sexual Object of the Nursing Period**.—However, even after the separation of the sexual activity from the taking of nourishment, there still remains from this first and most important of all sexual relations an important share, which prepares the object selection and assists in reëstablishing the lost happiness. Throughout the latency period the child learns to love other persons who assist it in its helplessness and gratify its wants; all this follows the model and is a continuation of the child's infantile relations to his wet nurse. One may perhaps hesitate to identify the tender feelings and esteem of the child for his foster-parents with sexual love; I believe, however, that a more thorough psychological investigation will establish this identity beyond any doubt. The intercourse between the child and its foster-parents is for the former an inexhaustible source of sexual excitation and gratification of erogenous zones, especially since the parents—or as a rule the mother—supplies the child with feelings which originate from her own sexual life; she pats it, kisses it, and rocks it, plainly taking it as a substitute for a full-valued sexual object.[2] The mother would probably be terrified if it

[2] Those to whom this conception appears " wicked " may read Havelock Ellis's treatise on the relations between mother and child which expresses almost the same ideas (The Sexual Impulse, p. 16).

were explained to her that all her tenderness awakens the sexual impulse of her child and prepares its future intensity. She considers her actions as asexually "pure" love, for she carefully avoids causing more irritation to the genitals of the child than is indispensable in caring for the body. But as we know the sexual impulse is not awakened by the excitation of genital zones alone. What we call tenderness will some day surely manifest its influence on the genital zones also. If the mother better understood the high significance of the sexual impulse for the whole psychic life and for all ethical and psychic activities, the enlightenment would spare her all reproaches. By teaching the child to love she only fulfills her function; for the child should become a fit man with energetic sexual needs, and accomplish in life all that the impulse urges the man to do. Of course, too much parental tenderness becomes harmful because it accelerates the sexual maturity, and also because it "spoils" the child and makes it unfit to temporarily renounce love or be satisfied with a smaller amount of love in later life. One of the surest premonitions of later nervousness is the fact that the child shows itself insatiable in its demands for parental tenderness; on the other hand, neuropathic parents, who usually display a boundless tenderness, often with their caressing awaken in the child a disposition for neurotic diseases. This example at least shows that neuropathic parents have nearer ways than inheritance by which they can transfer their disturbances to their children.

Infantile Fear.—The children themselves behave from their early childhood as if their attachment to their foster-parents were of the nature of sexual love. The fear of children is originally nothing but an expression for the fact that they miss the beloved person. They therefore meet every stranger with fear, they are afraid of the dark because they cannot see the beloved person, and are calmed if they can grasp that person's hand. The effect of childish fears and of the terrifying stories told by nurses is overestimated if one blames the latter for producing the fear in children.   Children who are predisposed to fear absorb these stories, which make no impression whatever upon others; and only such children are predisposed to fear whose sexual impulse is excessive or prematurely developed, or has become pretentious through pampering.   The child behaves here like the adult, that is, it changes its libido into fear when it cannot bring it to gratification, and the grown-up who becomes neurotic on account of ungratified libido behaves in his anxiety like a child; he fears when he is alone, *i. e.*, without a person of whose love he believes himself sure, and who can calm his fears by means of the most childish measures.[6]

Incest Barriers.—If the tenderness of the parents for the child has luckily failed to awaken the sexual impulse of the child prematurely, *i. e.*, before the physical determinations for puberty appear, and if that awakening has not gone so far as to cause an unmistakable breaking through of the psychic excitement into the genital system, it can then fulfill its task and direct the child at the age of maturity in the selection of the sexual object.   It would, of course, be most natural for the child to select as the sexual object that person whom it has loved since childhood with, so to speak, a suppressed libido.   But owing to the delay of sexual maturity time has been gained for the erection beside the sexual inhibitions of the incest barrier, that moral prescription which explicitly excludes from the object selection the beloved person of infancy or blood relation.   The observance of this barrier is above all a demand of cultural society which must guard against the absorption by the family of those interests which it needs for

[6] For the explanation of the origin of the infantile fear I am indebted to a three-year-old boy whom I once heard calling from a dark room: "Aunt, talk to me, I am afraid because it is dark." "How will that help you," answered the aunt; "you cannot see anyhow." "That's nothing," answered the child; "If some one talks then it becomes light." —He was, as we see, not afraid of the darkness but he was afraid because he missed the person he loved, and he could promise to calm down as soon as he was assured of her presence.

the production of higher social units. Society, therefore, uses every means to loosen those family ties in every individual, especially in the boy, which are authoritative in childhood only.

The object selection, however, is first accomplished in the imagination, and the sexual life of the maturing youth has hardly any escape except indulgence in phantasies or ideas which are not destined to be brought to execution. In the phantasies of all persons the infantile inclinations, now reënforced by somatic emphasis, reappear, and among them one finds in lawful frequency and in first place the sexual feeling of the child for the parents. This has usually already been differentiated by the sexual attraction, the attraction of the son for the mother and of the daughter for the father.[4] Simultaneously with the overcoming and rejection of these distinctly incestuous phantasies there occurs one of the most important as well as one of the most painful psychic accomplishments of puberty; it is the breaking away from the parental authority, through which alone is formed that opposition between the new and old generations which is so important for cultural progress. Many persons are detained at every station in the course of development through which the individual must pass; and accordingly there are persons who never overcome the parental authority and never, or very imperfectly, withdraw their affection from their parents. They are mostly girls, who, to the delight of their parents, retain their full infantile love far beyond puberty, and it is instructive to find that in their married life these girls are incapable of fulfilling their duties to their husbands. They make cold wives and remain sexually anesthetic. This shows that the apparently non-sexual love for the parents and the sexual love are nourished from the same source, i. e., that the first merely corresponds to an infantile fixation of the libido.

The nearer we come to the deeper disturbances of the psycho-

[4] Compare the description concerning the inevitable relation in the Œdipus fable (Traumdeutung, 2d edition, p. 185).

sexual development the more easily we can recognize the evident
significance of the incestuous object-selection. As a result of
sexual rejection there remains in the unconscious of the psychoneurotic a great part or the whole of the psychosexual activity for
object finding. Girls with an excessive need for affection and
an equal horror for the real demands of the sexual life, experience
an uncontrollable temptation on the one hand to realize in life
the ideal of the asexual love and on the other hand to conceal their
libido under an affection which they may manifest without self
reproach; this they do by clinging for life to the infantile attraction for their parents or brothers or sisters which has been
repressed in puberty. With the help of the symptoms and other
morbid manifestations, psychoanalysis can trace their unconscious
thoughts and translate them into the conscious, and thus easily
show to such persons that they are in love with their consan-
guinous relations in the popular meaning of the term. Likewise
when a once healthy person merges into disease after an unhappy
love affair, the mechanism of the disease can distinctly be explained as a return of his libido to the persons preferred in his
infancy.

The After Effects of the Infantile Object Selection.—Even
those who have happily eluded the incestuous fixation of their
libido have not completely escaped its influence. It is a distinct
echo of this phase of development that the first serious love of
the young man is often for a mature woman and that of the girl
for an older man equipped with authority—*i. e.,* for persons who
can revive in them the picture of the mother and father. Generally speaking object selection unquestionably takes place by following more freely these prototypes. The man seeks above all
the memory picture of his mother as it has dominated him since
the beginning of childhood; this is quite consistent with the fact
that the mother, if still living, strives against this, her renewal,
and meets it with hostility. In view of this significance of the
infantile relation to the parents for the later selection of the

sexual object, it is easy to understand that every disturbance of this infantile relation brings to a head the most serious results for the sexual life after puberty. Jealousy of the lover, too, never lacks the infantile sources or at least the infantile reinforcement. Quarrels between parents and unhappy marital relations between the same determine the severest predispositions for disturbed sexual development or neurotic diseases in the children.

The infantile desire for the parents is, to be sure, the most important, but not the only trace revived in puberty which points the way to the object selection. Other dispositions of the same origin permit the man, still supported by his infancy, to develop more than one single sexual series and to form different determinations for the object selection.

Prevention of Inversion.—One of the resulting tasks in the object selection consists in not missing the opposite sex. This, as we know, is not solved without some difficulty. The first feelings after puberty often enough go astray, though not with any permanent injury. Dessoir has justly called attention to the lawfulness betrayed in the enthusiastic friendships formed by boys and girls with their own sex. The greatest force which guards against a permanent inversion of the sexual object is surely the attraction exerted by the opposite sex characters on each other. For this we can give no explanation in connection with this discussion. This factor, however, does not in itself suffice to exclude the inversion; besides this there are surely many other supporting factors. Above all, there is the authoritative inhibition of society; experience shows that where the inversion is not considered a crime it fully corresponds to the sexual inclinations of many persons. Moreover, it may be assumed that in the man the infantile memories of the mother's tenderness as well as that of other females who cared for him as a child, energetically assists in directing his selection to the woman; while the girl, besides merging into a period of repression at the onset of puberty, is detained from the love for the same sex through the incitements of the competitor. The bringing up of boys by male persons (slaves in the ancient times) seems to favor homosexuality; the frequency of inversion in the present day nobility is probably explained by their employment of male servants, and by the scant care that mothers of that class give to their children. It happens in some hysterics that one of the parents has disappeared (through death, divorce, or estrangement), thus permitting the remaining parent to absorb all the love of the child, and in this way establishing the determinations for the sex of the person to be selected later as the sexual object; thus a permanent inversion is made possible.

SUMMARY

It is now time to attempt a summarization. We have started from the aberrations of the sexual impulse in reference to its object and aim and have encountered the question whether these originate from a congenital predisposition, or whether they are acquired in consequence of influences from life. The answer to this question was reached through an examination of the relations of the sexual life of psychoneurotics, a numerous group not very remote from the normal. This examination has been made through psychoanalytic investigations. We have thus found that a tendency to all perversions might be demonstrated in these persons in the form of unconscious forces revealing themselves as symptom creators, and we could say that the neurosis is, as it were, the negative of the perversion. In view of the now recognized great diffusion of tendencies to perversion the idea forced itself upon us that the disposition to perversions is the primitive and universal disposition of the human sexual impulse, from which the normal sexual behavior develops in consequence of organic changes and psychic inhibitions in the course of maturity. We hope to be able to demonstrate the original disposition in the infantile life; among the forces restraining the direction of the sexual impulse we have mentioned shame, loathing and sympathy, and the social constructions of morality and authority. We have thus been forced to perceive in every fixed aberration from the normal sexual life a fragment of inhibited development and infantilism. The significance of the variations of the primitive dispositions had to be put into the foreground, but between them and the influences of life we had to assume a relation of coöperation and not of opposition. On the other hand, as the primitive disposition must be a complex one, the sexual impulse itself appeared to us as something composed of many factors, which in the perversions becomes separated, as it were, into its components. The perversions thus prove themselves to be on the one hand inhibitions, and on the other dissociations from the normal development. Both conceptions became united in the assumption that the sexual impulse of the adult originates through the comprehension of the diverse feelings of the infantile life into one unit and one aspiration with one single aim.

We also added an explanation for the preponderance of perversive tendencies in the psychoneurotics by recognizing in these tendencies collateral fillings of side branches caused by the shifting of the main river bed through repression, and we then turned our examination to the sexual life of the infantile period. We found it deplorable that the existence of a sexual life in infancy has been disputed, and that the sexual manifestations which have been often observed in children have been described as abnormal occurrences. It rather seemed to us that the child brings along into the world germs of sexual activity and that even while taking nourishment it at the same time also enjoys a sexual gratification which it then seeks to again procure for itself through the familiar activity of "thumbsucking." The sexual activity of the child, however, does not develop in the same measure as its other functions, but merges first into the so-called latency period. The production of sexual excitation by no means ceases at this period but continues and furnishes a stock of energy, the greater part of which is utilized for aims other than sexual; namely, on the one hand for the delivery of sexual components for social feelings, and on the other hand (by means of repression and reaction formation) for the erection of the future sexual barriers. Accordingly, the forces which are destined to hold the sexual impulse in certain tracks are built up in infancy at the expense of the greater part of the perverse sexual feelings and with the assistance of the bringing up. Another part of the infantile sexual manifestations escapes this utilization and may manifest itself as sexual activity. It can then be discovered that the sexual excitation of the child flows from diverse sources. Above all gratifications originate through the adapted sensible excitation of so-called erogenous zones. For these probably any skin region or sensory organ may serve; but there are certain distinguished erogenous zones the excitation of which by certain organic mechanisms is assured from the beginning. Moreover, sexual excitation originates in the organism, as it were, as a by-product in a great number of processes, as soon as they attain a certain intensity; this especially takes place in all strong emotional excitements even if they be of a painful nature. The excitations from all these sources do not yet unite, but they pursue their aim individually—this aim consisting merely in the gaining of a certain pleasure. The sexual impulse of childhood is therefore objectless or autoerotic.

Still during infancy the erogenous zone of the genitals begins to make itself noticeable, either by the fact that like any other erogenous zone it furnishes gratification through a suitable sensible stimulus or because in some incomprehensible way the gratification from other sources causes at the same time the sexual excitement which has a special connection with the genital zone. We found cause to regret that a sufficient explanation of the relations between sexual gratification and sexual excitement, as well as between the activity of the genital zone and the remaining sources of sexuality, was not to be attained.

We were unable to state what amount of sexual activity in

childhood might be designated as normal—as activity which is not carried on at the expense of further development. The character of the sexual manifestation showed itself to be preponderately masturbatic. We, moreover, verified from experience the belief that the external influences of seduction might produce premature breaches in the latency period leading as far as the suppression of the same, and that the sexual impulse of the child really shows itself to be polymorphous perverse; furthermore, that every such premature sexual activity impairs the educability of the child.

Despite the incompleteness of our examinations of the infantile sexual life we were subsequently forced to attempt to study the serious changes produced by the appearance of puberty. We selected two of the same as criteria, namely, the subordination of all other sources of the sexual feeling to the primacy of the genital zones, and the process of object finding. The first is accomplished through the mechanism of utilizing the fore-pleasure, whereby all other independent sexual acts which are connected with pleasure and excitement become preparatory acts for the new sexual aim, the voiding of the sexual products, the attainment of which under enormous pleasure puts an end to the sexual feeling. At the same time we had to consider the differentiation of the sexual nature of man and woman, and we found that in order to become a woman a new repression is required which abolishes a piece of infantile masculinity, and prepares the woman for the change of the leading genital zones. Lastly, we found the object selection, tracing it through infancy to its revival in puberty; we also found indications of sexual inclinations on the part of the child for the parents and foster-parents, which, however, were turned away from these persons to others resembling them by the incest barriers which had been erected in the meantime. Let us finally add that during the transition period of puberty the somatic and psychic processes of development proceed side by side, but separately, until the normally acquired unification in the function of love has been established by the breaking through of an intensive psychic feeling of love for the innervation of the genitals.

The Factors Disturbing the Development.—As we have already shown by different examples, every step on this long road of development may become a point of fixation and every joint in this complicated structure may afford opportunity for a dissociation of the sexual impulse. It still remains for us to review the various inner and outer factors which disturb the development, and to mention the part of the mechanism affected by the disturbance emanating from them. The factors which we mention here in a series cannot, of course, all be in themselves of equal validity and we must expect to meet with difficulties in the assigning to the individual factors their due importance.

Constitution and Heredity.—In the first place, we must mention here the congenital variation in the sexual constitution, upon which the greatest weight probably falls, but the existence of which, as may be easily understood, can be established only through its later manifestations and even then not always with great certainty. We understand by it a preponderance of one or another of the manifold sources of the sexual feeling, and we believe that such a difference of disposition must always come to expression in the final result, even if it should remain within normal limits. Of course, we can also imagine certain variations of the original disposition that even without further aid must necessarily lead to the formation of an abnormal sexual life. We can call these "degenerative" and consider them as an expression of hereditary deterioration. In this connection I have to report a remarkable fact. In more than half of the severe cases of hysteria, compulsion neuroses, etc., which I have treated by psychotherapy, I have succeeded in positively demonstrating that their fathers have gone through an attack of syphilis before marriage; they have either suffered from tabes or general paresis, or there was a definite history of lues. I expressly add that the children who were later neurotic showed absolutely no signs of hereditary lues, so that the abnormal sexual constitution was to be considered as the last off-shoot of the luetic heredity. As far as it is now from my thoughts to put down a descent from syphilitic parents as a regular and indispensable etiological determination of the neuropathic constitution, I nevertheless maintain that the coincidence observed by me is not accidental and not without significance.

The hereditary relations of the positive perverts are not so well known because they know how to avoid inquiry. Still there is reason to believe that the same holds true in the perversions as in the neuroses. We often find perversions and psychoneuroses in the different sexes of the same family, so distributed that the male members, or one of them, is a positive pervert, while the females, following the repressive tendencies of their sex, are negative perverts or hysterics. This is a good example of the substantial relations between the two disturbances which I have discovered.

It cannot, however, be maintained that our notion of the structure of the sexual life is rendered finally complete by the addition of the diverse components of the sexual constitution. On the contrary, qualifications continue to appear and new possibilities result, depending upon the fate experienced by the sexual streams originating from the individual sources. This further elaboration is evidently the final and decisive one and the constitution described as uniform may lead to three final issues. If all the dispositions assumed to be abnormal retain their relative proportion, and are strengthened with maturity, the ultimate result can only be a perverse sexual life. The analysis of such abnormally constituted dispositions has not yet been thoroughly undertaken, but we already know cases that can be readily explained in the light of these theories. Authors believe, for example, that a whole series of fixation perversions must necessarily have had as their basis a congenital weakness of the sexual impulse. The statement seems to me untenable in this form, but it becomes ingenious if it refers to a constitutional weakness of one factor in the sexual impulse, namely, the genital zone, which later in the interests of propagation accepts as a function the sum of the individual sexual activities. In this case the summation which is demanded in puberty must fail and the strongest of the other sexual components continues its activity as a perversion.

Repression.—Another issue results if in the course of development certain powerful components experience a repression—which we must carefully note is not a suspension. The excitations in question are produced as usual but are prevented from attaining their aim by psychic hindrances, and are driven off into many other paths until they express themselves in a symptom. The result can be an almost normal sexual life—usually a limited one—but with the addition of a psychoneurotic disease. It is these cases that become so familiar to us through the psychoanalytic investigation of neurotics. The sexual life of such persons begins like that of perverts, a considerable part of their childhood is filled up with perverse sexual activity which occasionally extends far beyond the period of maturity, but owing to inner reasons a repressive change then results—usually before puberty, but now and then even much later—and from this point on without any extinction of the old feelings there appears a neurosis instead of a perversion. One may recall here the saying, "Junge Hure, alte Betschwester,"—only here youth has turned out to be much too short. The relieving of the perversion by the neurosis in the life of the same person, as well as the above mentioned distribution of perversion and hysteria in different persons of the same family must be placed side by side with the fact that the neurosis is the negative of the perversion.

Sublimation.—The third issue in abnormal constitutional dispositions is made possible by the process of "sublimation,"

through which the powerful excitations from individual sources
of sexuality are discharged and utilized in other spheres, so that
a considerable increase of psychic capacity results from an, in
itself dangerous, predisposition. This forms one of the sources
of artistic activity, and, according as such sublimation is complete
or incomplete, the analysis of the character of highly gifted, especially of artistically disposed persons, will show any proportionate
blending between productive ability, perversion, and neurosis. A
sub-species of sublimation is the suppression through reaction-
formation, which, as we have found, begins even in the latency
period of infancy, only to continue throughout life in favorable
cases. What we call the character of a person is built up to a
great extent from the material of sexual excitations; it is composed of impulses fixed since infancy and won through sublimation, and of such constructions as are destined to suppress effect-
ually those perverse feelings which are recognized as useless.
The general perverse sexual disposition of childhood can therefore be esteemed as a source of a number of our virtues, insofar
as it incites their creation through the formation of reactions.[5]

Accidental Experiences.—All other influences lose in significance when compared with the sexual discharges, repressions,
and sublimation; the inner determinations ,for the last two processes are totally unknown to us. He who includes repressions
and sublimations among constitutional predispositions, and considers them as the living manifestations of the same, has surely
the right to maintain that the final structure of the sexual life is
above all the result of the congenital constitution. No intelligent

---

[5] That keen observer of human nature E. Zola, describes in his book La
Joie de vivre, a girl who in cheerful self renunciation offers all she has
in possession or expectation, her fortune and her life's hopes to those
she loves without thought of return. The childhood of this girl was
dominated by an insatiable desire for love which whenever she was de-
preciated caused her to merge into a fit of cruelty.

person, however, will dispute that in such a coöperation of factors there is also room for the modifying influences of accidental factors derived from experience in childhood and later on. We may now continue with our task of enumerating the factors which have become known to us as influential for the sexual development, whether they be active forces or merely manifestations of the same.

Prematurity.—Such a factor is the spontaneous sexual prematurity which can be definitely demonstrated at least in the etiology of the neuroses, though in itself it is as little adequate for causation as the other factors. It manifests itself in a breaking through, shortening, or suspending of the infantile latency period and becomes a cause of disturbances inasmuch as it provokes sexual manifestations which, either on account of the unready state of the sexual inhibitions or because of the undeveloped state of the genital system, can only carry along the character of perversions. These tendencies to perversion may either remain as such, or after the repression sets in they may become motive powers for neurotic symptoms; at all events, the sexual prematurity renders difficult the desirable later control of the sexual impulse by the higher psychic influences, and enhances the compulsive-like character which even without this prematurity would be claimed by the psychic representatives of the impulse. Sexual prematurity often runs parallel with premature intellectual development; it is found as such in the infantile history of the most distinguished and most productive individuals, and in such connection it does not seem to act as pathogenically as when appearing isolated.

Adhesion.—The significance of all premature sexual manifestations is enhanced by a psychic factor of unknown origin which at present can be put down only as a psychological preliminary. I believe that it is the heightened adhesion of fixedness of these impressions of the sexual life which in later neurotics, as well as in perverts, must be added for the completion of the other facts; for the same premature sexual manifestations in other persons cannot impress themselves deeply enough to repeat themselves compulsively and to succeed in prescribing the way for the sexual impulse throughout later life. Perhaps a part of the explanation for this adhesion lies in another psychic factor which we cannot miss in the causation of the neuroses, namely, in the preponderance which in the psychic life falls to the share of memory traces as compared with recent impressions. This factor is apparently independent of intellectual development and grows with the growth of personal culture. In contrast to this the savage has been characterized as "the unfortunate child of the moment."⁸ Owing to the oppositional relation existing between culture and the free development of sexuality, the results of which may be traced far into the formation of our life, the problem how the sexual life of the child evolves is of very little importance for the later life in the lower stages of culture and civilization, and of very great importance in the higher.

Fixation.—The influence of the psychic factors just mentioned favored the development of the accidentally experienced impulses of the infantile sexuality. The latter (especially in the form of seductions through other children or through adults) produce the material which, with the help of the former, may become fixed as a permanent disturbance. A considerable number of the deviations from the normal sexual life observed later have been thus established in neurotics and perverts from the beginning through the impressions received during the alleged sexually free period of childhood. The causation may thus be divided into the responsiveness of the constitution, the prematurity, the quality of heightened adhesion, and the accidental excitement of the sexual impulse through outside influence.

⁸ It is possible that the heightened adhesion is only the result of a special intensive somatic sexual manifestation of former years.

The unsatisfactory conclusion which must result from an investigation of the disturbances of the sexual life is due to the fact that we as yet know too little concerning the biological processes in which the nature of sexuality consists to form from our isolated examinations a satisfactory theory for the explanation of either the normal or the pathological.

CONTENTS.

88 CONTENTS.

www.ingramcontent.com/pod-product-compliance
Lightning Source LLC
Chambersburg PA
CBHW051431270326
41934CB00018B/3475

www.ingramcontent.com/pod-product-compliance
Lightning Source LLC
Chambersburg PA
CBHW051431270326
41934CB00018B/3474